THE DINER

WHY IS CHURCH IMPORTANT?

SHANE SOWERS

Native Dogma Press

The Diner: Why is Church Important?

Copyright © 2014 Shane Sowers

Published by Native Dogma Press

All rights reserved.

First printing 2014

Scripture quotations are taken from the Holy Bible, New Living Translation, copyright ©1996, 2004, 2007, 2013 by Tyndale House Foundation. Used by permission of Tyndale House Publishers, Inc., Carol Stream, Illinois 60188. All rights reserved.

This book is a work of fiction. Names, Characters, places and incidents are either the product of the author's imagination or are used fictitiously.

ISBN-10: 150107332X

ISBN-13: 978-1501073328

DEDICATION

Lord Jesus, the head of the Church.

My beloved, Jeanine and my many blessings, Scott, Sean, and Shannon.

My loving family and friends all over the world.

My wonderful family at Central Baptist Church

Yes, everything else is worthless when compared with the infinite value of knowing Christ Jesus my Lord. For his sake I have discarded everything else, counting it all as garbage, so that I could gain Christ and become one with him. I no longer count on my own righteousness through obeying the law; rather, I become righteous through faith in Christ. For God's way of making us right with himself depends on faith.

Philippians 3:8-9

CONTENTS

	Acknowledgments	i
	PART 1- It is the Law	
1	The Sabbath	1
2	The Lord's Day	13
	PART 2 – You Need It	
3	The Invitation	27
4	Confession and Assurance	39
5	Reading the Word	55
6	Preaching the Word pt. 1	67
7	Preaching the Word pt. 2	89
8	The Lord's Supper	111
9	The Benediction	123
	PART 3 – Your Neighbor Needs It	
10	Meeting Together	135
11	The Family	149
12	Be the Church	165
	Conclusion	183

Can you combine serious biblical presentations on hotly disputed topics in a futuristic fictional context and make it work? I don't know, but Shane Sowers is brave enough to tread where most of us non-fiction writing, "prose is safe" writers fear to go! I really enjoyed Shane's witty and smart story. You'll be challenged at many points, but will want to stay on the journey to see what will happen next. A truly enjoyable means of engaging the Christian mind!

James White, director, Alpha and Omega Ministries

Shane Sowers goes underground to show us why church is important. The fascinating futuristic society beneath the surface of the earth is a surprisingly excellent setting for tackling many difficulties and failings within the church today. The book transcends denominations and is sure to benefit Christians of all walks by showing us why we ought to do what we are doing, and why we ought to do what some have stopped doing. The fresh new way that Shane communicates the problems and solutions for the church in this important work is the real upside.

Sye Ten Bruggencate, apologist, proofthatgodexists.org

This is an intriguing story that combines science fiction with godly truth. Easy to read, yet thought-provoking. I can't wait to read more!

Sheri Martin

ACKNOWLEDGMENTS

The members of Central Baptist Church for all of your love and support. Especially all of you who have been there since the beginning.

Dyna Ustare for all of your guidance.

Mom and Dad.

Jeanine.

Sheri Martin

My boy Steve, Dr. Oakley, Todd Morikawa, Steve Rost, Dr. T, Dr. J, Dr. K, Sye, Jason Meyer, Ken Jones and the White Horse Inn.

The Marrow Men

PART 1 – IT IS THE LAW

1 THE SABBATH

Jason Roland, with a tray of food in hand, sat at the end of a table for breakfast with his family. On the tray are scrambled eggs, bacon, pancakes and orange juice with a large cup of water. After he said grace, he began to eat with his two daughters Nancy and Grace and his wife of thirteen years, Cindy. He is a tech-welder by profession, with a goatee, broad shoulders and freshly shaven hair. He is said to be analytic and patient, extremely mild mannered and an excellent communicator.

As one of the elders of Salem Baptist Church, Jason spends much of his free time equipping the members of the church by visiting them house to house and patiently reasoning with them from the Holy Scriptures. While Jason ate with his family, Micha Jennings, a young member of Salem Baptist Church, sat down at the same table with a piece of bacon already in his mouth and a large smile.

Micha is a spacey yet intelligent young hacker, a student intent on getting upside to collect information from the mysterious people who live above. He continued to smile as he chewed the piece of bacon and looked Jason directly in the eyes. He waited with anticipation for Jason and his wife to ask him what had been going on in his life, but neither said a word. They only sat there returning little grins on their faces. It was as if they were waiting to see how long Micha could play his little game. *This is the Diner. It is the Law. You need it. Your neighbor needs it.*

Finally, Micha could not take it anymore and blurted it out…"I figured out how to get upside last night." Jason's wife giggled, and his children smiled.

"Here we go," Jason said. "You figured it out this time, huh?"

"Yes, and I know I keep saying this, but this time…I did it!"

Jason Roland paused and thought with a smirk, his arms folded, and eyes directly on Micha. "Ok we'll bite. Tell us how."

"Okay, check this out," Micha whispered. "I was searching through the web last night, and I hacked into the communication files of the Department of Development and Structure and read some of the messaging." Micha looked to the left and right. "So," he said, "what caught my attention was a tunnel that was accidentally dug leading to the East Wing of central and out to the upside. It's a tunnel out, Jason. I found it. So now, all I need to do is find out where it is, cut a hole through the wall and it will take me to the upside." Micha pumped his right fist and said, "Yes!" He sat back and took a bite out of another piece of bacon, smiling triumphantly as he ate.

Jason imagined the thousands who found refuge in elaborately developed and decorated underground facilities equipped with all that is necessary for survival. These people rejected the technological advancements in the realm above ground and later referred to this land above as "the upside." Incredibly, the modern dwellings that were created, with ornate paintings and decor coupled with digital images of never ending scenery from all over the world, would truly rival the caverns built by the "dwarves" in the old stories told by Tolkien. The whole compound was intricately encased in solid steel.

"Question, my friend," Jason said. "Since this whole compound is intricately encased in solid steel ten feet deep, just how exactly are you going to cut a hole through it?"

"Well, I'm still working on that," said Micha. "But that's not the real problem. The real problem is that I have to find out where the tunnel out actually is. It is somewhere in the East Wing, and I have to locate it before I can cut into anything. It could be anywhere in that wing, but,"—he looked right to left again—"I have a plan in the works. What I need to do is search for the tunnel out on the other end, follow it through to the steel wall, get the serial numbers and match them up inside the East Wing. Accordingly, I will have the tunnel's location then cut through the wall somehow. I will be free."

"But Micha," Jason said, "don't you have to get upside first to do this?"

"Well, yeah." Micha cocked his head. "How else will I be able to find the tunnel to mark the serial numbers? I have to find it first. Then I will know exactly where to cut, and I'll be able to get out."

"Um." Jason scratched his head. "But you will

already be out. Right? Why would you need to cut a hole in the wall to get upside when you are already upside?"

Micha looked up with his eyes pointing to the right side of his face and nodded slightly and thoughtfully. Just then, out of nowhere, a voice behind Micha said, "You know Micha, you have got to be the dumbest smart guy I know."

Jeff Lee is Micha Jennings' roommate at school. He is a bright, unshaven, and inquisitive young man studying electrical engineering. Jeff is interested in many things but keeps much of it to himself. He tends to be the voice of reason for Micha when there is slight oversight.

"You know," Micha said, "these are just minor problems. Not to worry. They are just little kinks in the chain. No need to panic."

"So anyway," Jason broke in and changed the subject, "we missed you guys in church last week."

"Yeah, I overslept," Micha said. "I was up for a while doing research Saturday night."

"You know," said Jason, "you all say that, but how can you oversleep on Sunday? You have to be here for breakfast in the morning. It's the law."

"Yeah, I know." Micha felt uncomfortable. "But after breakfast, uh, I went home, fell back asleep and, uh, slept through my alarm."

Jason looked at Micha with his left eyebrow higher than his right and a little smirk, making Micha a bit more uncomfortable.

"Hey Jason." Micha looked at Jason trying out his best puppy-dog face. "Can you just say 'okay' so I don't have to think of another lame excuse?"

"Fine. Okay."

"Come on Jason," said Micha, "it's not like I'm breaking a Law by not going to church. Right?" Both Micha Jennings and Jeff Lee looked at Jason Roland for an affirming look of approval. They didn't get one.

"No. Actually, you are."

"Okay, now I'll bite," Micha said. "Explain."

"Yes." Jeff Lee piped into the discussion. "Please explain."

"It's simple guys. Remember the Sabbath Day to keep it holy."

"Whoa, whoa, whoa. Wait a minute Jason." Micha interrupted laughing sarcastically under his breath. "We don't keep the Sabbath anymore. I thought we don't do the Sabbath thing. Isn't it all done?"

"Okay," Jason said. "Yes, there were changes with the Sabbath. Some of its particulars have truly passed away. However, the moral quality still remains."

"I'm listening," said Jeff.

"What you need to see when it comes to understanding the Law is how helpful it is for us to categorize it into three simple categories: The Moral, the Civil, and the Ceremonial." Jason took a drink of his orange juice and a bite of his pancakes dripping with strawberry syrup. He chewed quickly. "The moral Laws are those like the Ten Commandments. Thou shalt not kill, steal, and lie. Pretty simple.

"The civil Laws are those like making sure there is a railing around the roof of your house so that no one falls from it. These are similar to our Department of Development and Structure building codes today.

"The ceremonial Laws are like those of sacrificing goats and bulls for atonement of sin. So watch this.

The ceremonial Laws are no longer in effect because of the sacrifice of Christ on the cross. Following me so far?" Jason nodded his head looking at Micha and Jeff to see that they were still with him. They returned the nod and Jason continued. "But the civil and moral Laws still remain. The Ten Commandments are always in effect as well as the general equity of the civil Laws."

"General equity?" asked Jeff.

"Basically, general equity concerning the civil Laws are those like when the Israelites were commanded to put a railing around the roof of their house. This was, essentially, done to protect human life. Therefore, protecting human life is the general equity or the universal truth in the civil Law concerning the fastening of a railing around the roof of their house. This is what is important. It functions like the moral Law. You guys still following me?"

Both Micha and Jeff nodded their heads as they chewed their food.

"Now today," Jason said, "we do not normally have parties on the roof of our dwellings like they did in Israel, so we would not have a moral obligation to put a railing on the roof of our house. In light of this, what is important is the general equity of this Law. This Law was given to protect people who might fall off the roof during a gathering. The Law was squarely aimed at your responsibility for protecting human life in your dwelling place. For example, today, if you live in a high rise and you have a balcony, then, because of general equity, you would have a moral obligation to put a rail around the balcony to keep people from falling to their death. Protect human life in your house. The blood will be on your hands."

"Okay." Micha interrupted. "So let me get this straight. The ceremonial Laws are no longer for today because of the sacrifice of Christ. On the other hand, the general equity of the civil Laws and the moral Laws are still in effect today. What you are getting at is, essentially, if the Ten Commandments are still applicable today, then we would have to assume that since the Sabbath command, or the fourth commandment, is part of the Ten Commandments, then it still applies. Is this your point?"

"Yes sir."

"I guess that makes sense," said Jeff. "It is still wrong today to kill, to steal, and to lie, even though Christ fulfilled the Law. So why not the Sabbath? I think I'm getting it."

"But wait," Micha interjected. "All of this brings back to mind a conversation I had a bit ago with Jerry." Micha looked at Jeff to see if he remembered. "You remember Jerry from last semester?" Jeff nodded his head in affirmation. "Jerry said that the whole Law passed away after the death of Christ, and the only moral Laws that apply today are the ones that Christ reaffirms in the New Testament. He referred to it as 'Christ's Law'. At any rate, he also mentioned that the only Law that Christ did not reaffirm in the Ten Commandments was the fourth one, remembering the Sabbath. That is why he says that the Sabbath Law no longer applies today."

"That seems reasonable," said Jeff. "But,"—he looked at Jason—"but you don't agree."

"Alright." Jason continued. "First of all, the method he uses is wrong. We do not, nor cannot, say that all the Laws of God passed away and the only ones we are supposed to follow today are those reaffirmed by Christ. The method really should be the opposite. We should understand that all the Laws of God apply today and the only ones we do not follow are those Christ nullifies. Yes indeed, Christ did not remove the Sabbath Law.

"Secondly, even if your friend Jerry was right in his assessment, it still would not matter. Why? The Sabbath Law was given even before the Israelites arrived at Mount Sinai. Therefore, the Sabbath Law did not first appear with the Ten Commandments. It was clearly in place before the Laws of Moses were given at Sinai and was to be followed by, not just the Israelites, but every person. That is an important piece."

"Okay then," Micha said. "Well, if that is truly the case, then I guess I would agree. The whole argument would not even matter. What do you think, Jeff?"

"I would agree as well. Again, if it really is the case."

Jason smiled and motioned to his wife Cindy who reached into the bag next to her and pulled out Jason's Bible. He opened the Scriptures to Genesis. "We need to comprehend that from the very beginning there was something very special about this particular day. Genesis 2:3 makes it certain. God blessed the seventh day and declared it holy because it was the day He rested from all His work of creation. God made the seventh day holy. What this means is that He set the day apart and removed it from all that is common with the other six days. Clearly, this day is very different from the others. It is not a day like all the others because He made it Holy. Why do you ask? This is done for no other reason than for us to rest from our work and spend the whole day in worship of our God in memory of His rest from creation. In other words, He dedicated this day for worship. Since the creation of the world, God made it plain that this day of worship is to be set aside for us to worship Him and it is to be set aside by all creation which means everyone must keep it. It is a lot like the directive for all humanity to be fruitful and multiply. It means everyone. The Sabbath is a directive for all humanity to rest from their work and dedicate a day in reverent worship to the Lord. Again, for a human being to disobey this Law is to break the command of God, at all times and by all people. It is clearly breaking the Law."

Jason then turned in his Bible to the book of Exodus. Micha looked at Jason in eager expectation with Jeff at his side, smiling as he ate his last piece of bacon.

"And another thing," Jason said, "we see that before the Israelites even got to Mount Sinai to receive the Ten Commandments, they were already observing the Sabbath. In Exodus 16:23, as they were on their way to Mount Sinai, we see that the people were directed to daily gather manna to eat. Nevertheless, on Friday, they were to collect double the amount of manna because the next day was to be a Sabbath to the Lord.

> *He told them, "This is what the LORD commanded: Tomorrow will be a day of complete rest, a holy Sabbath day set apart for the LORD. So bake or boil as much as you want today, and set aside what is left for tomorrow." (Exodus 16:23)*

"And how can this be, unless the Sabbath Law was already in effect before they got to Sinai."

Micha and Jeff nodded their heads in thoughtful affirmation. Cindy began to clean up her daughters' trays, and Jason continued to make his case.

"You see," Jason continued, "before the ceremonial Laws and the Ten Commandments were even set up, they were already following the Sabbath directives. The Sabbath is not a ceremonial Law that passed away. Even when the Ten Commandments were given, in the fourth commandment, they were instructed to 'remember' the Sabbath day and keep it holy. Moses repeats the reason for that in the creation account of Genesis 2:3. And how could this be if it was not already in effect and already known? Interesting here, did you notice, even the 'stranger or sojourner' in your gates is to observe this commandment.

"Now watch this. We could generally understand this person to be a Gentile visitor or, more simply, a foreigner. Do you see that the directive is that even they are to follow the fourth commandment? Furthermore, we should remember that for Passover Gentiles or foreigners are not to be a part of it; it was forbidden. Why are the Gentiles to follow the Sabbath but not Passover? It seems to indicate that this is a command to be followed by both Jew and Gentile.

"Therefore, disobeying this command is to break the command of God. It is breaking the Law. If you want, we could look at how all of the men of God before Moses consecrated the seventh day. We could also look at the historic records to witness Sabbath observance among the Gentiles in their own countries. We would find that they actually consecrated a day every week to worship, and in many cases, this was, believe it or not, Saturday.

"This clearly shows us, my brothers, that it is the Law that is written on our hearts made clear in Romans 2:14-15. So there you have it. The Sabbath was not part of the ceremonial aspects of the Law, and neither was it first introduced in the Ten Commandments. Everyone everywhere knows it and are held accountable to it. The Sabbath does not pass away. It could not pass away. Technically, we say that this Law is a creation mandate."

The horn to conclude the time for breakfast sounded, and people everywhere began to clean up. Jeff started to eat faster.

"What is a creation mandate?" Micha asked.

"It is, basically, a mandate that God gave all of mankind when He created them. We are to have dominion, be fruitful and multiply, and keep the Sabbath day holy."

"So," said Micha, "I guess what you are saying is that not going to church to worship God really is breaking the Law of God. Why didn't you just say that in the first place, Jason?" Micha laughed and sat back in his seat with a look of satisfaction on his face.

However, Jeff Lee did not seem as satisfied. As Jason and his family continued to clean up, he asked, "So, Jason, can we meet up again for lunch today? I just got one more question, but I want to think about it a little. Time's up in here anyway."

"Of course, Jeff. You are always welcome to eat with us. I'll do my best to answer your question."

Jason and his family went to discard their recyclables, for everything in Salem is recyclable.

And, as the entire Roland family walked to the exit, Micha and Jeff both looked forward deep in thought as they started to clean up their area.

Jeff said, "You do know, Micha, that it's also against the Law to try to find a way upside. Right?"

2 THE LORD'S DAY

Lunch in Salem is an anticipated time for the labor-force. All work in must immediately cease when the meal horn sounds, and all people must file into *the Diner* to eat. It is Salem law. Underground, food and water are limited and precious, and the reality of this particular universal need has forced Salem to set regulations for the commodities. All food and water are cultivated, manufactured, stored and distributed by the governing body of Salem, and is illegal, punishable by death, to possess any form of consumables not created and dispensed by the governing body. In addition, by Salem law, all citizens must go to the food dispensaries to receive the consumables and eat three meals a day, every day. Citizens must eat the three meals. The regulations state that everyone must report to the dispensaries to receive nourishment without exception, unless, of course, there is just and reasonable cause. One reoccurring problem is an ever increasing list of what is considered "just and reasonable cause" by the governing body of Salem. Many of the decisions tend to be relative to the person and the details of the cause. Hence, some people have, over the years, become suspicious of wrong doing when these exceptions are made. As a result, suspicions have caused doubt that the governing body judges indiscriminately, and for some, confidence in leadership is low. Nonetheless, they are constantly reminded that the other option, the upside, would be much worse. The reminder of why they are in the underground has been able to keep uprisings and rebellions at bay for several years, and no one here wants the alternative. Moreover, citizens believe in the very essence of what it means to be human. Man should not be merged with machines; it is unnatural. Man should not become progressively more synthetic; it is unnatural. The people underground have even referred to the people upside as "syners," a play on the word "synthetic," and an implication what they really think of those above. Life upside is considered unnatural by the people below. Accordingly, those underground have rejected most technologies but have embraced those that they deem as "having dominion" over the earth.

    Jason Roland and his family sat at a table with Jeff and asked the Lord's blessings. Today for lunch, Salem is serving a favorite, grilled ham and cheese sandwiches with freshly made potato chips. As soon as Jason finished the prayer, another voice in the group said "Amen." Standing with tray in hand behind Jeff was Micha Jennings. *This is the Diner. It is the Law. You need it. Your neighbor needs it.*

    "Hi everyone," Micha said. "There was no way I was gonna miss this."

"You are always welcome to eat with us, Micha," said Cindy Roland.

"Okay, Jason." Jeff jumped in with his Bible already opened and asked his much anticipated question. "So how are we to handle the Scripture in Colossians 2:16-17?

So don't let anyone condemn you for what you eat or drink, or for not celebrating certain holy days or new moon ceremonies or Sabbaths. For these rules are only shadows of the reality yet to come. And Christ himself is that reality. (Colossians 2:16-17)

"It mentions 'a Sabbath' as one of the things that are a 'shadow of things to come' and we see that it is Christ who is that reality. Does it not seem that this Scripture is saying that the Sabbath is a ceremonial law that passes away with the work of Christ?"

Jason took a look in his Bible at the passage of Scripture. His lips pursed and his finger tapped on the table as he read. There was silence with only the sound of the chewing of food, the swallowing of water and the rumble of hundreds of other conversations in *the Diner*. Just then, a smile appeared on Jason's face as he laid his Bible down on the table and took a bite out of his sandwich. With food still in his mouth, he shifted it all into his right cheek and said, "Okay."

He then put his finger up signaling Jeff and Micha to hold on and chewed quickly. He finally swallowed and continued. "What the Apostle Paul is referring to here are the ceremonial Sabbaths that we find in the book of Leviticus. Within chapter 23, namely verses 23-38, there are parts that make a real distinction between the seventh day Sabbath and the Sabbaths that have to do with the ceremonial feasts and offerings. If you were to look again and compare, much of what is mentioned in Colossians 2:16-17 is also mentioned in Leviticus 23. The ceremonial Sabbath feasts were truly types and shadows of the work that Christ did on the cross and now, we have that reality in our Lord Jesus. The Scriptures make it clear that there are more than just one kind of Sabbath. Truly, we find a distinction between the Sabbaths here in Leviticus and the seventh day Sabbath or what we would call the 'Christian Sabbath' today. In Colossians, they are ceremonial feast Sabbath's that have, indeed, passed away."

"Okay, I think I'm okay with that," said Jeff. "You know, what you made very clear, is how interesting all of this works together in the Scriptures. The way the Old Testament and New Testament work together is genius. It's brilliant." Jeff Lee sat and thought a bit more, looking like he had something else to ask.

"You got another question Jeff?" Jason asked.

"As I was thinking about this earlier, I thought about something you said concerning the categories of the Law. The moral, civil, and the ceremonial, I believe."

Jeff moved around in his seat to give himself what seemed to be a better position to launch his question. "Okay," Jeff continued. "I was wondering, have you had anyone mention that the categories of the Law are not shown explicitly in the Scriptures and so we should not categorize the Law as moral, ceremonial, and civil? In other words, the Bible does not directly tell us that we should categorize the Law this way. You follow?"

Micha Jennings quickly looked at Jason and

wondered how exactly he would answer this question.

"No worries. I get this question all the time," said Jason. "The reason we do this is to help us understand what the various Laws have as their end. Another way to put it is that it helps us to understand the Laws of God better. It aids us in identifying which Laws have passed and which one's are still binding. It aids us in knowing the difference between dietary Laws and the sacrificial system from the moral Laws to which we are bound forever. We cannot throw it all out. We discussed this earlier. You guys remember?"

Micha and Jeff nodded their heads in approval as they chewed.

"Okay then," Jason said. "To further demonstrate, much of the Law is moral and the moral Laws of God, such as the Ten Commandments, are a representation of the moral character of God, and it reflects who He is and what He desires. For example, it's like our mothers growing up. They have certain things they want from us, and most of it reflects who she really is. I had a mother who was a 'clean freak,' and she wanted everything clean without ever tolerating a mess. Notwithstanding, growing up we understood that it was not necessarily a general characteristic for mothers to be 'clean freaks', but it was one that was specific to our mother. My friend's mom allowed us to be messy when we played at their house. Not so with my mother. I found that it was a part of my mother's character, and the rules I had growing up, reflected this. In any case, we need to know that God does not change. Therefore, we need to know that these Laws, then, are forever binding on us because they will never change. God will never change. His character will never change. What He desires morally will not change. It won't be right one day and then be wrong another. It cannot be thrown out. You guys following me so far?"

Again, Micha and Jeff nodded their heads in approval as they continued to eat their sandwiches.

Jason continued, "As we study the Scriptures, we find that some of the Laws are specific to the time and context of the people of Israel and are categorized into what we call the civil Laws. These expired; however, the general equity of these Laws may apply today, morally. The ceremonial Laws came as a shadow for a time and expired. And again, the moral Laws are reflections of God's character. Take, for instance, my friend's father. He is the director of Salem and was a soldier. He will only be the director of Salem for two years, then his term will expire. He will lead us and point us in the right direction in Salem, just like the ceremonial Laws pointed us to Christ but are now expired. He was also a soldier, yet, he is not currently active in protecting us from our enemies foreign and domestic. The skill he has as a soldier may be needed; however, it is only in a certain context, where he will need to protect us again, and ergo, the general duty of protecting life is still active in him. Maybe not as a soldier specifically, but as a citizen, generally, he will protect us. This is like the civil Laws. They don't apply directly to their initial context, but the general idea of the laws still apply in certain situations. Finally, my friend's father will be his father forever. It is who he is, and it will never change. This is like the moral Laws. Now, are these clear categories identified specifically by the Holy Scriptures? No. Nonetheless, it is what we do to help us understand the Laws better."

"Hmmm." Jeff pondered. "You know, I think I got it now. But how then are we to understand Hebrews chapter four? Does this passage not teach that Jesus is our rest. We cease from our evil works and enjoy a Sabbath rest in being a Christian. Jesus is our rest."

"The whole teaching concerning the Sabbath in chapters three and four have been interpreted in many different ways, and the way you interpreted it, is surely one way to understand it. However, the best way to conceptualize this teaching, is that of a future rest in heaven. The author of the Hebrews showed us that there was a rest given in the Scriptures at the time of creation and at the time of Joshua. However, the author showed that there was still a rest that remained for us to enter, yet we will enter only by faith. This is the rest of heaven, and this rest will not be enjoyed by anyone in unbelief. That is the warning. But because there is this warning, it doesn't mean that the Sabbath rest of creation is no longer to be followed. We still keep the Lord's Day till we go to heaven."

Jeff finished his lunch and moved his tray to the side, clasped his hands together, put his arms on the table and looked Jason Roland directly in the eyes.

"Okay," Jeff said. "I just got one more important question."

Jason smiled in a way that would suggest that he knew exactly what it was that Jeff would ask him.

Jeff asked, "The Sabbath is actually the seventh day. After everything you said, I understand the moral nature of the law, but then why do we observe it on the first day of the week instead of the seventh.

Why on Sunday instead of Saturday?"

"Yup, knew it was coming." Jason chuckled. "We worship on the first day of the week in memory of the resurrection of our Lord Jesus, just like the Sabbath was in memory of God's rest from creation. It is called the 'Lord's Day.' Think about it like this. The resurrection is like a new creation and it accomplished new creations." Jason quoted 1 Corinthians 5:17 from memory.

This means that anyone who belongs to Christ has become a new person. The old life is gone; a new life has begun!

"This is a nice picture relating to the creation of the world where God rested on the seventh day. The new creation happened on the first day of the week, so that is why we celebrate and rejoice on that day. Therefore, we must understand that it is no longer the seventh day, but the first day.

"Two things to clear this up. First of all, even though we do not have a clear and emphatic statement making this specific change, we have enough evidence in the Scriptures to conclude that the change took place. The Scriptures indirectly show the change from the Jewish Sabbath to the Christian Sabbath referred to as the Lord's Day. The apostles seemed to have made this change with all the rights and authority given to them by Christ Himself. Not to mention, Christ is the 'Lord of the Sabbath' and it is His divine right to change the day from the seventh to the first. We also see in Deuteronomy 5:15 the principle of remembering salvation.

Remember that you were once slaves in Egypt, but the LORD your God brought you out with his strong hand and powerful arm. That is why the LORD your God has commanded you to rest on the Sabbath day.

"We see that a reason other than resting from our labors to remember and glorify God in light of His creation, is resting from our labors to remember our Lord's mercy, grace and power in delivering us from sin just like the Israelites rested to remember their deliverance out of Egypt. This picture of deliverance was a foreshadow of the deliverance of Christians through the work of Christ's strong hand and powerful arm. This is truly fulfilled. But there is still the point of remembrance. We remember and rejoice in our salvation on the day Christ rose from the grave, the first day of the week."

Jason opened his Bible to the book of Acts.

"Acts 20:7. This shows us that the believers, with Paul, met together on the first day of the week to observe the Lord's Supper, which is, of course, part of our worship services.

On the first day of the week, we gathered with the local believers to share in the Lord's Supper. Paul was preaching to them, and since he was leaving the next day, he kept talking until midnight. (Acts 20:7)

"This shows us that there is a change happening from the Jewish Sabbath to the Christian Sabbath, with the Jewish Sabbath on Saturday and the Christian Sabbath on Sunday or the Lord's Day."

Jason flipped the pages of his Bible to the book of 1 Corinthians.

"In 1 Corinthians 16:1-2, Paul desires the church to take up offerings on the first day of the week.

Now regarding your question about the money being collected for God's people in Jerusalem. You should follow the same procedure I gave to the churches in Galatia. On the first day of each week, you should each put aside a portion of the money you have earned. Don't wait until I get there and then try to collect it all at once. (1 Corinthians 16:1-2)

"This implies that this is the time the believers would be gathered for worship. Historically, it was common practice of the Jews to take up a collection on the Sabbath in their gatherings in the synagogue. Collections being taken up seems to suggest that they were all gathered in a meeting, and it is at this time, the first day of the week, that Paul desired the collections to happen."

Jason immediately flipped the pages of his Bible to the book of Revelation.

"In Revelation 1:20, the apostle John uses the term the 'Lord's Day' and most scholars would take this day to mean Sunday.

It was the Lord's Day, and I was worshiping in the Spirit. Suddenly, I heard behind me a loud voice like a trumpet blast. (Revelation 1:20)

"This is where we get our terminology of the 'Lord's Day' as it pertains to Sunday morning worship."

Micha and Jeff nodded their heads in understanding.

"Secondly," Jason said. "We see throughout church history, since even the first century, that Christians have gathered for worship on the first day of the week calling it the 'Lord's Day.' This is the Christian observance of the moral commands of the Sabbath. The Christian Sabbath. As you can see, it is not as straight forward as many would like, but with careful study, we can easily demonstrate the moral demands of the Sabbath and the change from Saturday to Sunday. Nevertheless, with all the work

THE DINER: WHY IS CHURCH IMPORTANT?

needed to make this conclusion, I can see how there would be confusion with this subject. Yet, at the same time, I do think it is so obvious, that the Scriptures really seem to assume that we know this already."

Jeff asked, "Jason, where did you learn this stuff? Did you go to Seminary?"

"No. I just go to church every week." Jason laughed, winked his right eye and said, "Hint. Hint."

"I guess you don't want to go to Seminary for nine years," said Jeff.

"Well, only those upside go to Seminary that long. They got three years of combat training to go along with three years of academics and three years of field training. Down here, Seminary is only three years. No matter, I just don't have the time. Plus, you need to be handpicked these days. I just don't fit the demographics. Actually, I don't think I even know what they are."

"Well, either way," Jeff said. "You were definitely able to help me out with this."

After that, Jeff put his hands around his head and leaned back in his chair with a smile. He breathed a sigh, almost one of relief or at least a moment of decompression.

Micha Jennings waited for the right moment for him to share a revelation that he had earlier that day. "You know, after breakfast this morning, I went back to my study and did further study." He laughed. "It has been a while since any subject other than trying to find a way upside has become passionate for me. I was struck by Jesus' words in Mark 2:27 showing us that the Sabbath was made for man not the other way around. What jumped out at me was that his words imply that the Sabbath is something that is to be a benefit for man. Again, it is here for us and not the other way around. So, since the creation, God gave us this day to worship Him for our benefit. We don't want to miss out on what He gives to us, do we? All of this has made me appreciate where I live. I recognized what and who I have in my life and how they are all wonderful gifts of God. I am so concerned about the awesome possibilities of what is up there when I should cherish the awesome things I have here in front of me. I need not find blessings up there, I already have them down here."

"Nice job Micha," said Jason.

Cindy agreed. "Yeah. Really good work. I'm impressed."

"Me too," Jeff said.

As everyone finished their lunch and cleaned up, there was a moment of satisfied silence among the group with smiles all the way around.

But then, Jason's daughter Nancy said, "Hey Dad. If we don't go to church isn't it a sin?"

"Well, yes my dear."

Jeff Lee said, "I agree."

"Same here," said Micha.

"If that's true," Nancy said, "why do you believe that it's a sin? Don't you gotta be breaking some command in order for it to be a sin? Right?"

The group looked at each other in silent wonder. Jeff Lee grimaced with a grin as he tapped his forehead and chuckled. Jason Roland smiled with a gleam in his eye, and Micha Jennings looked bewildered with jaw on the table.

"You know what, Nancy," Micha said. "Why didn't you just say that in the first place."

The whole group laughed.

Cindy hugged her daughter and said, "That's my girl!"

PART 2 – YOU NEED IT

3 THE INVITATION

Louis Lopez, with a dinner tray in his hand, walked to the counter to get a cup of water and additional hand towels. Louis has long been the Pastor of Salem Baptist Church. Immediately after seminary, he married Julia, and nine months after the wedding, they had Marshall. Marshall is now eighteen years old and a student at Salem University studying philosophy, just like his dad did before he went to seminary. The first five years of pastoring for Louis was a difficult one, stretching him to the brink and relieving him of his vain youthful ambitions. He came to the all important realization that the nature of the church is to be a family, not a business. Furthermore, he understood that he was entrusted with the spiritual well-being and development of Kings and Queens of the Kingdom of Heaven. Louis is an obvious extrovert, athletic build with a full beard and piercing eyes. He was blessed with a good sense of humor and is always up for a good laugh. Naturally, he is the type of pastor to repeatedly mention that a cheerful heart is good medicine.

As Louis walked to the counter to get some water, he was met by Charlie Walker, a middle aged and recent widower who lost his wife in a construction accident almost a year ago. Charlie has had difficulty moving forward in life and is dealing with frequent bouts of depression. He stays busy during the daytime regulated hours as a dental assistant. Nevertheless, at night, the pain is difficult. *This is the Diner. It is the Law. You need it. Your neighbor needs it.*

"Hey there, pastor," Charlie said, "may I join you for dinner this evening?"

"You may. So, what do we got for dinner tonight? Looks like meatloaf and mashed potatoes."

They both walked to the dining area to join the rest of the Lopez family.

"Hey," said Louis. "So you ever wonder where they get meat for the meatloaf?"

"What do you mean?"

"Well, have you ever seen any cows down here?" Louis inquired.

Charlie laughed. "You know, I just don't think about it. Its better that way."

"Everyone says that, but I have the hardest time not thinking about it. I mean, what about steak night? You know I heard that they are cloning steak. Can they do that? Just clone a piece of steak, without cloning the cow?"

Charlie shrugged his shoulders.

"Well," Louis said. "I guess if they can clone people, why not steak?"

"It has to be the case. I don't see chickens around either."

"True that," Louis said. "Well, whatever it is, it is

deemed good for us by the head honchos, so it doesn't matter. We are all going to eat it. Period. And another thing, I always find I have to remind myself that because of all the potential for sickness and disease down here, they will not give us anything deemed bad for us. No more 'junk food' as the founders used to call it."

It was found that skipping meals caused speedy malnutrition and a weakened immune system, subjecting the person to sickness and diseases potentially harmful to the community of Salem. The governing body, under the direction of the Department of Health, infused the necessary vitamins and vaccines into the food. Three times a day, every day, thousands of people would come to be nourished and immunized with all the consumable necessities of life in halls resembling the high school cafeterias of old.

"Hello," Charlie said sarcastically. "I think that makes not knowing where the stuff comes from a little better."

Louis expressed, "I think the point is, it is what we need, not what we want. It's like our church these days. We get what we need, not what we want. I don't know if you know this, but it was the case years ago that churches were concerned with giving the people what they wanted, instead of what they needed. Many can only speculate as to why they did this. Nevertheless, it is my understanding that it caused the 'Great Apostasy of 2040' which we read about in our church history classes. Again, we get what we need. The key word…Need."

Louis Lopez and Charlie Walker sat down with Louis' family. They bowed their heads as Louis asked the Lord to bless their meal. As they ate their dinner, Louis noticed a tear fall from the left eye of Charlie's slightly bowed head. His heart went out to him because he couldn't imagine the pain and suffering that losing a wife could cause a man. Louis and his family remained silent out of respect for the grieving that their friend and brother was experiencing. Eventually, Charlie looked up, wiped the tears from his face and smiled.

"You know," Charlie said. "Every day I keep thinking that this is the day the pain will disappear. I think, this is it, and I will be able to move on from this day forward. However, after the day is over it feels like nothing has changed. Nothing is different. It is like a knife is piercing my heart through my bed mattress as I lay down, twisting over and over again. Pretty morbid huh? It is times like these when I wish I was upside. I hear that the *syners* have a program that can change moods and emotions with a simple digital command. Not only can the LINC system in their bodies heal physical wounds, but it can also heal emotional ones. It can even alter our memories. I could use some of that now." Charlie Walker paused till he regained even more composure. "You know what, I'm really sorry for talking like this, I don't really mean it. Just feeling sorry for myself, I guess."

"Hey." Louis was overwhelmed with sympathy. "We can't say that we completely understand the pain you must be experiencing, but we want to be here for you. Okay? Consider yourself invited to eat with us whenever you want to, whether you are feeling good or bad. We love you, care about you, and we want you to feel welcome to eat with this family, always. You are invited."

"Yes," Marshall said. "You are always invited, my man."

Julia smiled and nodded her head in approval.

"Well," Charlie said. "I guess sometimes I feel like I need to be around people, but I feel awkward inviting myself. Anyway, thank you for inviting me to be with you all. In this culture, I realize the honor it is to be invited to eat with a family in *the Diner*. I know I am blessed. It is good to feel wanted."

"Good," Marshall said. "Cause you are a blessing to us. We want you around."

"I don't know why." Charlie's voice sounded like he had a lump in his throat.

"Just cause you are you," Marshall said. "You are my brother in Christ. I don't need anymore reason to love you and see you as a blessing. That is it."

"Charlie," Louis said. "Remember that Christianity is about family, not business. Some in the past have run it that way, but we eventually got this straightened out with the help of the twenty-first century teaching of the *9 Marks of the Healthy Church* by Mark Dever. When it comes to the Lord, we are invited. We all have the need deep down inside to feel wanted by others. To know that you are welcomed into the presence of the Lord is a big deal. With the invitation, we feel wanted by God."

"Like you said," Marshall adds, "in Salem, the honor you feel when you are invited to be with a family during a meal is fulfilling. In the same way, the Creator of the universe is inviting you to be in His presence with His family on Sunday, the Lord's Day. You have an invitation from the Lord Himself. He wants you."

Louis said, "You know, this is essentially what we

call the 'call to worship' in our church services. It is the declaration of God's invitation for us to turn from our worldly distractions and focus our hearts, minds and actions to reverence and worship of our Lord Jesus."

"Dad, I think Psalm 100:1-5 is a good place to see this. Can I read it?" Marshall asked.

Louis Lopez nods his head, and Marshall opened his Bible and read the passage:

Shout with joy to the LORD, all the earth! Worship the LORD with gladness. Come before him, singing with joy. Acknowledge that the LORD is God! He made us, and we are his. We are his people, the sheep of his pasture. Enter his gates with thanksgiving; go into his courts with praise. Give thanks to him and praise his name. For the LORD is good. His unfailing love continues forever, and his faithfulness continues to each generation." (Psalm 100:1-5)

"So essentially," Charlie adds, "we have a call to come into the presence of God to worship Him. It is our invitation. He wants us to be with Him."

"Yeah," said Marshall. "But an invitation from the Creator of the universe. Our awesome and almighty God. How can you beat that?"

"It is Christ who is calling out to us," Louis said. "He is inviting us into His house. He is inviting us to come before Him, turning away from everything else and joining His redeemed people to praise Him and give Him all He deserves. We need to get it in our heads, let us always remember, that church is not the place where we invite Him to join us."

"Ok, you lost me there," said Charlie.

Louis said, "Sometimes we have the mentality that we are gathering together in the church building, and we are inviting the Holy Spirit to come to us so we can give Him what He wants, our worship. We come to church to invite the Holy Spirit to be with us. To be fair, this is not necessarily intentional on the part of some. However, it can make things a bit confusing and rob us of the genuine impact of Christ's invitation. The Creator of the universe, who owns it all, is inviting you to come to His house, not our house, to receive all the blessings He wants to give to us through His servants, His ministers."

Louis' voice rose as if he was somewhat irritated. He said, "We think we have invited Him and laid out our table, plates and silverware to have Him come to our house so we can serve Him. It is the other way around. Our Lord Jesus wants to serve us. He wants to serve us His Invitation, His Forgiveness, His Table, His Word and His Blessings. This is not our world, this is our Father's world. We don't invite. He does. We want to show God that He is wanted by us, but more importantly, we need to know that we are wanted by Him."

"Wow." Charlie seemed very surprised. "That sounds so different. I think we feel like we go to church to serve Him, not the other way around. I guess that is why we feel guilty when we don't go. We are not giving Him His due. When in reality, we are the ones not receiving what He wants to give. But isn't that the issue right there."—his face looked downcast again—"I mean, He is the Creator of the universe, He does not serve us, we serve Him. Don't we? It feels so wrong to think that He serves us."

Louis nodded his head in affirmation. "Yeah, it is understandable. But watch this. John 13 gives us the account of Jesus washing the feet of the disciples. He got up from the table, took off his robe, put a towel around his waist, poured water in a bowl, and washed the feet of the disciples. This is significant. Tradition shows us that feet washing was a task considered to be so vile that the host of a meal would not even allow his Jewish slave do it. It was the job of the Gentile slave. Now this is the task being done by Jesus for his disciples. It is understandable why Peter, knowing this, responded the way he did."

"I remember," Charlie said. "He was like, wow, are you serious? No way Lord, you will never do this. I won't allow you to stoop so low as to do this awful and vile thing.'" Charlie paused and thought for a minute. He sat up in his chair, nodded and smiled as if he understood.

He continued, "Wait. So, what you are saying is that we are essentially doing the same thing here. We will not allow God to serve us in church. Serving us is not His job. It is our job to serve Him. We don't want Him to stoop so low."

"Exactly," said Louis. "Now remember, Jesus said that if Peter did not let Him wash his feet, then Peter would have no part of Him. Christ came not to be served but to serve. This is the radical nature of the Kingdom of God. He is asserting that the King will rule by servant hood, not by lording it over his subjects. The great must be a servant. The first must be slave of all. This is the way of the Son of Man."

Marshall jumped in, "So dad, it makes sense why many of us don't want to go to church. We really don't understand what is happening. We should love and enjoy our Lord, but instead we are here out of duty, punching a time card to show a record that we did our weekly service. Ironically, we are missing the point, and we should be trying to break down the walls of the church to get in on Sunday to receive the wonderful things the Lord is giving. But I guess, on second thought, maybe, what God is giving us on Sunday is not what we are wanting or maybe we just don't think He is giving anything to us on Sundays. Its like we think we go to church to do our duty, pay homage to our Lord, to give our offerings, to hear a lecture on religion, and basically, act like we are religious people. But in reality, Jesus wants us to feel the privilege of his invitation to worship, to receive the forgiveness of Christ, to hear our assurance of salvation declared, to respond to God with psalms, hymns, and spiritual songs, to receive the means of grace, baptism, the Lord's Table, and the Word of God preached. He wants to serve us and give us what we need. He wants to give us everything the world cannot give to us. Again, its like we think going to church is like going to work or going to school. No wonder we don't like going to church. Who wants to go to work on the weekend." He shrugged his shoulders and laughed. "Church is not like going to work. It is more like going to someone's house for dinner, or in our case, inviting someone to come and sit with you to eat at *the Diner*. We have an invitation. We are wanted. Think about it, how would you feel if you invited a person to come and sit with you and they said, 'Nah, I'm going to sit over there instead. It's too boring at this table.' Would we not consider it rude? Would it not make the person who invited feel unimportant? Not going to church is a lot more like this illustration than we may think."

"Yes," Louis said, "and furthermore, like the food here at *the Diner*, we get what we need, not what we want. What if we were only to eat what we wanted like candy, milkshakes, ice-cream, fried foods, fast processed foods? We would not be healthy. Heart disease, diabetes, cancer, lethargy, headaches, sickness, and disease would be in our future. It's the same with church. We would be malnourished and weak Christians if we only got a diet of nothing but the things we want. Our Lord knows what we need. So then, we come into his presence to receive all He desires us to have for life and life more abundantly. It is what He says we need."

"There aren't churches that actually do that. Right?" Charlie asked.

Louis said, "I don't know for sure here in the entire Network or on the upside, but there was a host of them in the twenty-first century. It is probably what caused the 'Great Apostasy of 2040' where hundreds of thousands of professing 'Christians' walked away from both the church and the faith after a severe economic depression and the illegalization of Christianity in 2039. When real struggles and persecution hit the church at large, they could not withstand the turmoil, lost what hope they had, and walked away."

"Wow," Walker said. "That's a scary thing. I guess it is important to be a healthy Christian so that we will be able to stand when times get rough. We are to be strong in the Lord (Ephesians 6:10)."

"That is essentially the whole message of the book of Hebrews," Louis adds. "Christianity has much to do with suffering. It is part of walking with Christ and being found in Him. We do feel overwhelmed at times. Furthermore, it feels like we have way more than we can handle in life and … you know what?"

Louis paused for a few seconds to build every-ones anticipation. "It is true. We cannot handle it." Louis paused again to give them time to reflect. "But we, as Christians, are not supposed to handle it. We are supposed to walk trusting in God and knowing He is our strength and nothing else. We need to know that either He will help us handle life or He will sit us down so we can watch Him handle it for us. In the Scriptures, it is not uncommon for Him to tell his people to stand and watch Him bring them the victory. Truly, we can overcome the world because Christ has overcome the world. He knows that we bring Him glory when He brings us through the impossible. It is not about the glory of us overcoming the difficulty. It is about the glory of Christ bringing us through the difficulty. He is, then, so glorified. We grow, He is glorified. We stand, He is glorified. We overcome, He is glorified. It is not us, but Christ through us. He is glorified because He is doing His work in us. We can take no credit. The beauty of Christianity is not about what we do for Him, but what we believe He has done for us. I love it. Sorry bro. I get"—he pumped both fists in the air—"excited talking about this."

Charlie Walker began to understand the importance and joy of the invitation we receive from God to enter into His presence to receive of His wonderful grace. He saw that Christ desires to serve us His grace, so that we may grow healthy in the grace and knowledge of our Lord, bringing Him the glory He so richly deserves. He now understood that he is wanted by the Creator of the universe.

"This changes everything doesn't it," Charlie said.

"Everything," said Marshall.

"Well," Charlie said, "Now I just gotta figure out how to cope better when I am alone." He laughed. "I need to find some time to laugh, I guess. Nothing seems to make me laugh these days."

"Well," said Louis. "You are a dental assistant. Right? Use some our your laughing gas." Lopez laughed.

Julia interjected, "Louis!"

In medicinal laughter, they all cleaned their areas and walked over to dispose of their recyclables. As they walked toward the dispensary doors, they received a retinal scan for identification and a body scan to confirm consumption for the evening. All the information is stored in the highly secure mainframe of Salem

4 CONFESSION AND ASSURANCE

In Salem, every-time a person walks out of *the Diner*, he or she is scanned for identity and physical health. The data are collected and analyzed by the Department of Health and delivered to the citizens with instructions. Many times, as they leave, the attendant will instruct them that they need to report to the Department of Health because they were found to be deficient. The citizen will report to the clinic in the Department of Health wing and receive a supplement injection. Sometimes, the citizen will be brought into the evaluation office to find out he or she has a more serious problem. Some are told that they are having problems, and the clinic will continue to monitor progress and give instructions concerning permitted and restricted daily activities. Others are told that they have a non-contagious terminal condition and an estimate of how long they could expect to live. However, they will not have that long. Those with this particular diagnosis have sixty days to get their affairs in order and report back to the

Department of Health for general hospice care. In such cases, they will receive treatment for pain and anxiety as they are withheld food and life sustaining medical attention, all within a place the people call *Paradise*.

Food supply and supplements have been deemed too precious to give to those who will not survive for a reasonable length of time, over five years to be exact. Of course, this has always been a difficult practice in Salem, and it has been challenged by a few. However, the reality of limited food supply and supplements cause the majority to see its necessity and accept it as the way of life underground.

Jessica Mitchell received such a report thirty days ago. She wiped the tears from her face and took a deep breath before she walked into *the Diner* for breakfast. Jessica came to meet her boyfriend, Marshall Lopez, the son of Louis Lopez, with the intention of finally telling him of her plight. She currently attends Salem University and is studying formal logic hoping to work as a tech for Research and Development.

Jessica Mitchell is an attractive young student, musically gifted in singing and playing the guitar. She sings on the worship team at Salem Baptist Church every weekend alongside Marshall on percussion. Jessica and Marshall have been dating for the past two years and spend much of their free time with each other. She was afraid this meeting would change everything, and it did. She walked up behind Marshall. *This is the Diner. It is the Law. You need it. Your neighbor needs it.*

"Hello my sweet man. What's for breakfast?"

"It looks like waffles and bacon," Marshall said.

THE DINER: WHY IS CHURCH IMPORTANT?

"Looks like lots of orange juice today too. You know, I heard some of the old timers say that the early pioneers frequently said that the bacon here tastes weird. But since I was born here, how am I supposed to know?"

"Yeah, I hear that, too," she said. "It tastes normal to me."

"Me, too."

Jessica and Marshall both sat down at the table, and Marshall asked the blessing. Unusually, Jessica ate her food rapidly, getting Marshall's attention.

"So Jessica, you hungry this morning?" Marshall laughed.

"Just eager to finish my food this time so I don't get reprimanded again," she said. "It was embarrassing to be escorted out by security forces last time."

"Yeah, I have noticed that you have not been eating all of your food lately. My darling, you need to get all of that nourishment or else you're gonna get really sick."

Jessica cried. Marshall reflected back on everything he had just said wondering what it was that caused the tears. Many thoughts raced through his mind as he waited for Jessica to get her composure. He wondered if she called him here to break up with him. Marshall sat back in his chair with his appetite dwindling.

"Jess," he said. "What's wrong? You're kinda freaking me out."

"I need help, I am really scared. I need to confess something to you."

Marshall's teeth clenched, and his jaw muscles pulsated. His appetite was totally gone as he put down his fork and wondered what she did.

Jessica said, "I feel so bad because I have not been honest with you. I have been so scared to tell you because of what this could mean. I am so sorry. I do love you with all of my heart, and I'm afraid that you will cast me away after you find out. I guess it was selfish of me."

Surprising to Marshall his defensiveness softened, and he lovingly reached out to Jessica and took her by her trembling hand.

"You can tell me," he said. "I love you. We can work it out. We always do."

"Not this time." Jessica's throat cracked and more tears fell from her eyes.

"What do you mean?" he said.

"Marshall, I'm dying. Thirty days ago I was told that I have lung cancer, and that I have less than five years to live. They said it is probably due to radon poisoning." Jessica squeezed Marshall's hands, and with sorrow in her heart, she said, "They're sending me to *Paradise*."

"Wait," he said. "You said thirty days ago. Jess, that means you only have thirty days left."

Marshall broke down and cried. Jessica got up from her chair and moved around to the other side of the table to sit next to Marshall. She held him as the full weight of despair crushed his spirit.

In Salem, conversations like this happen all the time. They are not making a scene or attracting attention to themselves. This is life down in Salem, the life they have all come to know. Marshall got enough of his composure to speak.

"Jess, so maybe we can go back and talk to the department and see if they made a mistake or something."

"Come on, Marshall. You know that will not do any good. Once the decision is made, it's final, and there is no negotiating. It is the law. Even if they made a mistake, I would still have to go. You know it can't be changed."

"There has got to be something we can do," said Marshall.

"Yes there is. We can have the best thirty days of our lives together."

Marshall smiled a little as he remembered why he fell in love with her. He remembered how she always tried to make the best of every situation.

"Marshall," she said. "I don't want to waste anymore time trying to make more time. You know how this will go and what happens to people when they go down that road. I spoke to one of them yesterday, and he said his real regret was using the last moments with his wife trying to beat the system instead of spending the time enjoying one another. After the talk, I decided not to be afraid to tell you anymore and to enjoy our last days together. I was not sure after my confession that you could assure me you cared, and I think that was my biggest fear. I guess I wanted reassurance that I would be reassured somehow. I'm so sorry."

"Jess, don't be sorry. I love you with all of my heart. And I can understand why you would be afraid. It has to be such a confusing thing. This,"— he had the look of confusion—"you know this is just all so difficult to grasp right now." Marshall continued to wipe tears from his face. "I can't imagine how you must feel. I think the fear of rejection surely would be a difficult one to control. I know one thing for sure, be assured, I'm not going anywhere. I promise."

"Thanks Marshall. I needed to hear that."

"You know," he said, "I think we all need to hear that. We need reassurance that we will be reassured. We need to hear that we will hear that we will be okay. I bet that sounded confusing." Marshall laughed. "That is why in our services we are committed to take a moment to do 'confession and assurance.' We take the time to confess our sins to our Lord and hear a declaration of his forgiveness. We are reassured. We need to hear it."

"Yeah," she said, "that's another fear I have. I'm worried about what will happen to me after I die. Am I really forgiven? Am I really going to be with Christ in heaven? I feel doubtful sometimes because I am reminded of all the bad things I have done and I am afraid of the possibility of being rejected by God. I can't help but wonder how is it even possible that He could love me. It's just to good to be true. You know what I mean?"

"I think so," he said. "You know I hear my dad talking about this all the time and it all just became so today. I wonder if the reason we don't want to confess our sins is because we don't want to be reminded of our fear of the reality of rejection. We cannot comprehend how it is possible that we would not be rejected. We become so afraid of the possibility of the eternal consequences for sin that we miss the declaration of assurance given immediately after. And interestingly, not just rejection from God, but rejecting ourselves, which in turn, will cause us to doubt our very salvation. We cannot believe God forgives us because we can't forgive ourselves. We know that we would never forgive us if the tables were turned. Therefore, the declaration of assurance falls upon deaf ears. In addition, we just don't want to be reminded of our sins because we don't want to be reminded just how sinful we really are. But in reality, sometimes we just can't ignore the sin. We are up all night thinking about it, needing to deal with the tremendous guilt and fear of rejection from ourselves and more importantly, God. This is why we need to hear and believe the assurance of our salvation."

"That's a good point," she said. "In some ways, I think that much of my problem is because of my rejection of myself. I think that because I can't forgive myself, how in the world will God forgive me. I doubt His forgiveness because I can't imagine God loving me more than I love myself. I judge myself instead of realizing that God is the Judge who loves me. I know the Bible declares that I am forgiven and God forgives me, in Christ, but I think the real issue is that I don't forgive myself for the things I have done. But the sad thing is I, apparently, care more about what I feel than what God declares. It's like idolatry. I am the real god in my life, and that is why what I feel matters more." Jessica paused and then whispered, "Jesus, I'm so sorry for my unfaithfulness and idolatry. Please forgive me. Lord have mercy on me."

"Amen," Marshall said. "You know my dad always quotes a reformed theologian when he says that our hearts are 'idol factories.' We make idols out of everything, even ourselves. Idols lead us to doubt the love and the Word of God. Nonetheless, we need to know. You need to know. You are forgiven, and you are a child of God. That is what makes the

Gospel so wonderful. He can do what we cannot do and can forgive us when we cannot forgive ourselves. He would even die for His enemy which is something we just can't imagine doing ourselves. This is the promise from a God who does not lie. Christ died for our sins according to the Scriptures and he was raised on the third day according to the Scriptures (1 Corinthians 15:3-4). He came into the world to seek and save that which was lost." (Luke 19:10).

Marshall opened his Bible to first John.

He said, "1 John 1:9 says,

But if we confess our sins to him, he is faithful and just to forgive us our sins and to cleanse us from all wickedness.

"There is forgiveness for us when we sin. When sin abounds, grace abounds even more (Romans 5:20). As far as the east is from the west so far does he remove our sins from us (Psalm 103:11-12). Be assured Jess. You are forgiven. You are the righteousness of God in Christ Jesus."

"Ok, but, how do I know that I am one of His children?" she asked.

"Do you sincerely believe that Jesus is the Christ, the Son of the living God?"

"Yes."

"Well," he said. "If you really believe that, then you are a child of God. If you weren't a child, you would not believe it. It's that simple."

"Well then how do we know for sure that all this is for real?" she asked.

"Because our God said it is, and that's all we need."

"Yeah, but what evidence do we have? He needs to prove it right? We need more than just the Bible.

I mean how do we know that the Bible is even the Word of God?"

He said, "Because the Bible says that it is."

"Marshall seriously. Don't you think that you need to prove it?"

"You can't prove it." Marshall leaned back in his seat waiting to see how Jessica would respond.

Jessica said nothing, but her facial expressions showed that she was deep in thought. Her lips pursed and her eyes rolled to the upper right side of her face looking as if she was trying to access something. She also took a hand towel and wiped her fingers one at a time.

"Look," he said. "The Bible is the authority and foundation of all truth. All things are proven true because the Bible proves it true. It is our authority and foundation. The question is, can there be anything under the foundation of our house?"

"No," she said "Because if there is something under it, it would not be the foundation, the thing under it would be."

"Right. So if the Bible is our foundation, there can be nothing holding it up or it would not be our foundation. If we use scientific evidence to prove the Bible true, then the scientific evidence becomes the foundation. That is why I say you can't substantiate the Bible. It is our axiom."

"By axiom, you mean a self-evident truth that is the starting point for all reasoning?" she asked.

"Right. Besides that, how can we prove what actually came from the mind of God? Unless He reveals it, we won't know. And we also have to trust He is telling the truth."

"Go on."

"Okay. Let me ask you a question. Did you dream last night?" he asked.

"Yes."

"What did you dream about?"

She said, "I dreamt that you and I were walking around the giant reservoir in Salem. You and I were discussing what songs we were going to do for worship and, a water monster was standing there playing the guitar as an accompaniment for us."

Marshall laughed. "Okay. Well, I don't believe you. You need to prove to me, with evidence, that you had that dream last night."

"Now how in the world am I gonna do that?"

"You see!" he exclaimed. "You can't. Either I believe you or I don't."

"I see. Okay. So that changes lots of things."

"Look at it this way, let's say it is all inconclusive. What else are you going to turn to? You got any better options besides Christ?" he asked.

"No," she said. "I guess not. Okay, but you said that I would not believe if I was not a child of God. Right?"

"Right." said Marshall. "We were all born in sin and are prone by nature to hate God and our neighbor. It is in our very nature to rebel against God. Additionally, it is not that unbelievers do not believe that God exists, it is that they don't believe that He is good. It is not that they don't believe, but they won't believe. Romans chapter one makes that abundantly clear. If you love Him, have faith in Him, and see the Kingdom, then you have been 'born again.' You are a child of God. You are a Christian. Awesome huh?"

"Yes. I guess it's just hard to imagine because we

still sin."

"Yeah, but, sinning is still a reality for us," he said. "Paul the apostle makes it clear in Romans chapter seven, but all is not lost. We will continue to grow and mature by the power of the Holy Spirit, and continue to die to ourselves and be made more and more like Christ. Its the doctrine of Mortification and Vivification. You can read about it later. For His children, He promised to complete the work He started in us.(Philippians 1:6) For that, we can truly rejoice. He will finish His work in us. But, let me also add that we cannot rest our assurance on our works and sins, it has to be based on our faith in God's Word. Our assurance must not be based on our efforts, but on what God declares in his Word. We receive by faith and by faith alone."

"But, she said. "Don't we have to make our calling and election sure?"

"Right. But why is it that we always go straight to our works?"

"I don't know what you mean, isn't that what we are supposed to do?"

Marshall answered, "Our works brings us nothing from God, but it is faith that is the instrument by which we receive from God. Why is it that we immediately jump to what we do when it comes to assurance instead of what we believe? Why is it our works that determines our maturity, instead of our growth in grace and knowledge? If it is by my efforts that I am assured of salvation, then I will never be assured. They are imperfect and tainted with sin, and always up and down. As a result, I am truly assured only because God declared that there is no condemnation for those who are in Christ Jesus

(Romans 8:1) and I believe I am in Christ Jesus. It is not what I do, but what I believe. That is why we need to hear the declaration of assurance from the very Word of God. Do we believe it?"

"Okay, but does not our good works also assure us of our salvation?"

"Yes, but maybe not in the way you might think."

"Go on."

"Our works assure us of our salvation because we see evidence that the Holy Spirit lives in us. We see the fruit of the Spirit in our lives. We look not at our works as our work, but as Christ's work in us in union with Him. I am assured I am a Christian, not because of what I am doing, but what we see the Holy Spirit doing in me. Again, union with Christ. Think about it. If we have an issue with greed we are then instructed that this behavior is not and cannot be that of a believer. And, if you continue to do this, then you will end up in hell because no one who does these things will inherit the Kingdom." Marshall opened his Bible to the book of 1 Corinthians. We read in the Scriptures,

Don't you realize that those who do wrong will not inherit the Kingdom of God? Don't fool yourselves. Those who indulge in sexual sin, or who worship idols, or commit adultery, or are male prostitutes, or practice homosexuality, or are thieves, or greedy people, or drunkards, or are abusive, or cheat people—none of these will inherit the Kingdom of God. (1 Corinthians 6:9:10)"

"Is that not a good point? That seems to be what it is saying," she said.

"Couple of things. First of all, how are we supposed to fill these categories? We are told that those who are greedy will not inherit, but how many times do you have to be greedy to be considered greedy? Some imply that if you keep doing it, you will eventually become those who are greedy. But if you look at the other vices in this Scripture, how many times do we need to commit adultery for you to be an adulterer?"

"Yeah, that is a good point. One time. Wow, it makes judging hard."

"Here's the point of it all. It's easy when it is applied to unbelievers, but for Christians, it becomes difficult to apply. I believe the apostle in this passage of Scripture declares something very different."

"What do you mean?"

"The passage continues,
Some of you were once like that. But you were cleansed; you were made holy; you were made right with God by calling on the name of the Lord Jesus Christ and by the Spirit of our God. (1 Corinthians 6:11)

"As Christians, we were washed by the blood of Jesus. We used to be that, but no longer."

"Secondly, when we are done hearing the erroneous council of some, we then make it a point to stop being greedy because we are afraid that if we keep doing it, we will not go to heaven. So we walk out determined. However, little do we know that even if we succeed we still sinned."

"Really? How so?"

"Because our motive for obedience is based on unbelief. We moved because we were afraid of being condemned after God assures us that there will be no condemnation for us in His Word. We moved thinking it is by our efforts that we will be kept from hell and not by our faith. In other words, we are being obedient to earn heaven by works and slip into the world of works righteousness. Let us not deceive ourselves this way. To act this way, is to act in unbelief and this is sin at its very core. What is in our hearts also plays a role in our obedience. Without faith it is impossible to please Him. So even in 'obeying,' we are sinning."

"That is a different way of looking at it," she said.

"I wonder if we even realize that to doubt our assurance in Christ is unbelief. Thinking that we may be in jeopardy of not being saved, losing our salvation or being condemned is unbelief in the promises that God has given. The simple act of doing good works because we are afraid that we may not be Christians, and that by doing them we can be assured is doubt of the worse kind. God made promises and if we do not believe them then are we not sinning? He promised that He gives eternal life, we will never perish and no one will snatch us out of His hands (John 10:28). He promised that He will never reject us (John 6:37). He promised that everyone who calls on the name of the Lord will be saved (Acts 2:21). He promised that the good work He began in us will be finished (Philippians 1:6). Do we believe it?"

"Yes, but the real question is are we really a Christian because these promises are for His people. Are we really Christians?"

"Right, but how is it that we become Christians? By works? Or by faith? John 20:31 says:

But these are written so that you may continue to believe that Jesus is the Messiah, the Son of God, and that by believing in him you will have life by the power of his name.

"It is clear that God wants us to be assured of our

salvation and the assurance is from His Word, not our works, and if we are not assured then are we not in unbelief? If God promises that all who call on Him will be saved and we are not sure that this is really the case, then what are we saying about God? He cannot be trusted. Unbelief. I called upon Him and He promised that I will be saved, and so all of these promises belong to me. I am assured because God is not a man that He should lie (Numbers 23:19), and His promises are truly Yes and Amen (2 Corinthians 1:20). Our assurance is in the promises of God, not our performance."

"I guess that means we always need to experience the forgiveness of Christ and his grace through the Word."

"Yes," he said. "That is why we have a time of 'confession and assurance' every week and are truly committed to it. You can be reassured that you will be reassured at church. We confess our sins and hear the declaration from the Word of God that we are forgiven and assured of our salvation through Christ. After the whole week of sinning and the deception of the world, we Christians, need to be reminded of the wonderful news that our sins are covered by the work of Jesus on the cross, and that's all we need. We need assurance, declared by the pastor, from the very Word of God. We cannot, must not, find our assurance in our works or the changes in our behavior over the course of our lives. We can be deceived by this and despair. Therefore, we need to hear it from the Word of God alone, and if we can't believe and be assured from the Word of God alone, then we will not, nor cannot, have assurance at all. If we don't listen to Moses and the Prophets then neither will we listen, even if someone rises from the dead (Luke 16:31). The declaration of forgiveness from the Word of God is our assurance."

"I remember that passage of Scripture," she said.

Jessica's eyes gleamed, and she smiled as Marshall finished speaking to her. The tension of emotions were gone. Jessica was breathing as if the weight of the world just fell off of her shoulders. She reached for Marshall and lovingly took his hands in hers.

"I feel a lot better now, Marshall. Being reminded of God's promises is truly reassuring. I truly do believe in Christ and the promises in His Word. I believe that all He said is true, and all He did really happened. Thank you for talking with me. And thank you for sharing the truth of God's Word."

"Of course."

"Oh my, I will truly miss our conversations. I will truly miss you, Marshall."

"I still can't believe it. I am really going to miss you as well."

"Let's have a really good time for the next thirty days, okay?" she asked. "I've got lots of money to spend. I just emptied out my entire savings. This is a good way for us to decompress. You interested?" Jessica laughs.

Suddenly, Marshall's eyes lit up. "I just thought of something… Will you marry me?"

5 READING THE WORD

Daniel Taylor, the pastor of Salem Presbyterian Church, stood in line with his wife, Michelle, and his two teenaged twin children, Isaac and Ashley, for lunch. He graduated seminary at the top of his class, and was immediately offered a position as an assistant professor. He turned it down to be the pastor of Salem Presbyterian, and has been there for the past twenty-two years.

Daniel is known for being a bit socially awkward at times and difficult to engage in real meaningful conversations concerning life in general. Many assert that he so brilliant, that most cannot understand what is going on in that mind of his. He knows it too, which makes it even more awkward. He is tall and thin with bright white hair and beard, wearing the famous blue t-shirt that he wears every-time he eats at *the Diner*.

Even though it can be difficult to communicate with Daniel about most things, he can communicate theology and biblical concepts in a surprisingly easy way for the average person to understand. He is also known for being one of the best preachers of his generation, and has been referred to as this generation's John Piper.

Daniel Taylor and his family sat down at the table, and he asked the blessing over their meal. After the prayer, there was another voice saying, "amen," with them.

"Spaghetti with meatballs for lunch today. Can I join you guys?" asked Victoria.

"Please do," Michelle answered.

Victoria Kelly is a single mother trying to raise her teenage son who sat with his friends at the far end of *the Diner*. Victoria works at the Department of Geo-Studies as an analyst for Drill Team 5, who have the responsibility of finding water for the Salem reservoirs. Her husband James passed away five years ago from radon-induced lung cancer. After his death, she went back to Salem University to finish her degree in Geology.

Over the years, communities like Salem not just survived, but thrived. Governing systems were in place with its powers of enforcement and defense, set up for the holistic well-being of the people. The citizens of Salem worked respectively within their specific fields of service, according to their individual skill-set, all for the comprehensive meeting of the physical needs in the community. Victoria Kelly is playing her role in the drama. After the tragedy, however, Victoria Kelly's son Zach never fully recovered from the loss of his father and has hardened his heart toward God, family, the church, and ultimately, Salem. Victoria is all out of answers. *This is the Diner. It is the Law. You need it. Your neighbor*

THE DINER: WHY IS CHURCH IMPORTANT?

needs it.

"So how is everything with you these days?" asked Daniel.

"That is a big question. You sure you want an answer?" Victoria replied.

"Well, since you put that way, I'm not sure now." Daniel Taylor laughed.

Michelle Taylor elbowed her husband in the ribs and gave him a stern look.

"Oops sorry," Daniel said. "Yes. We do want an answer."

"No, that's okay. It's not going that great, but I won't bore you with the details."

"Thank you." Daniel laughed again.

"No!" Michelle exclaimed. "Don't,"—she elbows Daniel in the ribs again—"listen to him. We do want to hear the details. Things not going so well with Zach?"

Daniel with a disgruntled look, whispered to Michelle, "I was just kidding around."

"You know it seems like there is so much going on down here and so much said. It is almost like I don't know what is true anymore. I don't know who to believe. I hear from scientists, doctors, and psychologists, concerning Zach and I can't make sense out of anything they say. It almost seems as if they don't even know what to do. They are just as much in the dark as I am. I guess they, at least, don't agree with each other."

"Is it like they know what is going on, but they don't really know what is supposed to go on?" Daniel asked.

"I would say that sums it up perfectly."

"That is one of the huge limitations of those

disciplines," Daniel said. "Especially, psychotherapy. They do a good job telling you why you are doing what you are doing, but they really can't say what you are supposed to be doing. I like to say it this way. They can tell you what 'is,' but they cannot tell you what 'ought.' Moreover, we are inundated with such information that have accumulated over the years comprising of observations and discoveries of what we are and why we are here, yet no one really knows for sure."

"They sure seem to talk like they know for sure," Victoria said, with a bit of sarcasm.

Daniel laughed. "Now don't get me wrong. What we, as mankind, have created and developed is spectacular and mostly have full control over it. Furthermore, what mankind has actually created and developed is so admittedly magnificent, that we have even amazed ourselves into overconfidence. Think of all that is reportedly being created and developed upside. Honestly, I never thought man would be capable of such things. Be that as it may, there is still so much before us that we still don't fully comprehend and have not been able to comprehend for some time.

"For instance, evolution has assumed that the more we are, as biological creatures, reduced to our very cells, the simpler we would appear. It was suggested, that once we were stripped down to the smallest parts, we would be made up of simple protoplasm. On the contrary, DNA was discovered and an entire universe of untapped information was waiting to be analyzed. As a result, we find that the more we seem to progress, the more it is shown that we know very little about our world. In other words, the deeper we go, the more we realize how much deeper we still need to go."

"So are we at a loss? Can we even know what is true?" Victoria asked.

"Do you remember back at the University, you had the humanities core classes for your undergrad degree?"

"It was a while ago, but I remember some of it."

"Do you remember lectures about truth theories in the Logic Module?" Daniel asked.

"Yes. I remember it damaged my brain."

"Yes,"—he laughed—"truth theories can be very complex and yet, after all that work, it still comes up wanting."

"What do you mean by 'wanting?'" Victoria asked.

"Well," said Daniel. "There is so much needed to comprehend theories like pragmatism, coherence, deflation, and correspondence theories, but they all seem to come up way short in being able to give a definitive definition for truth."

"Wait," Victoria objected. "I thought that the correspondence theory was the winner. It defined truth as that which corresponds to reality. The things that are true are found to be real in the world."

"Yes," Daniel replied. "It is the leading view today, but it is, in my opinion, because it is the most intuitive, or better yet, the most 'common sense' view. The problem, however, concerns reality. For example, snow is white if and only if snow is white. The question that needs to be asked is, 'is snow really white?' You familiar with the term Epistemology?"

"Yes," Victoria said. "It is the study of how we know things. Where and how we get knowledge, I think."

"Right," Daniel said, with surprise. "Nice job. So do you remember the difficulty we can have with principles like perception?"

"I do remember that."

"Good. So, we make judgments about an object we see, observe, and collect data. At any rate, we have a fundamental problem with knowing, from perception, direct or indirect, of what is real and what is not real. This has been an ongoing debate for some time.

"For instance, if we look at an ordinary pencil, it looks straight. But if we were to put it in water, now it looks crooked. If we look at the end of a straight road, it looks like it ends, but it doesn't. If we look at train tracks it looks like they become one track at the end, but we know they don't. This is what we perceive, but after more observation and evaluation, we find it is actually not the case. This is the essence of the problem. The question is, 'what if we cannot evaluate it?' We could check our perceptions in the cases I just gave. However, what about those things we can't verify? What of those we can't observe and evaluate? Did we perceive it correctly? How do we know, if we can't check? If we can't verify that it is real, then we can't say that something corresponds to reality, if we are not sure of the reality. Can we?

"Take for instance, a man and a woman are sitting at a table. The woman cries. Now, we could say that he must have said something that upset her, and would then conclude that what we witnessed was an unfortunate circumstance between the two. We believe this because when people are sad they cry."

"Yes," Victoria said. "But that's not the only reason people cry. She could have been crying because she was happy."

"Absolutely," said Daniel. "Now, let's say that after we discussed it, we turned toward the couple to find out the reason and they were gone. How are we supposed to find out what really happened? We cannot ask them to verify what it was that we perceived, and in this situation, what exactly was the reality? What was the truth? All we know is what might be the case. For all we know, she might have been sad because he was breaking up with her, or she was happy because he asked her to marry him. She might have been sad because he told her about a friend who just passed away in the clinic, or he told her of a wonderful memory he had of his dad and it touched her heart. We don't know for sure, and that's the essence of the problem, yet we can sure act like there really isn't one.

"What is more, all we are talking about is a simple conversation between a man and a woman. How much more uncertainty of what is in our universe, the underground, the human body, the mind, human behavior, or what it is that we ought to do when we never created ourselves. Sometimes, we can't even know what really, 'is,' so how are we supposed to know what 'ought' to be."

"But Daniel," Victoria said. "We cannot operate that way. I just can't believe that God wants us to live that way. Living life not knowing that things are true."

"You are right," Daniel responded. "God does not want us to live that way. That is why He gave us the Bible. That is where we get the 'is' and the 'ought.'"

"The Bible is our truth then?" Victoria asked.

"That is actually"—he put his hand on his Bible—"how I define truth. When it is asked, 'what is truth?,' I respond by saying, 'the 66 books of the Bible.' You see, the only possible way we can know truth, in all or even some things, is if someone who has comprehensive knowledge of everything, tells us. That's it. That is the only possible way for us, human beings, to know what is really true in this world. Therefore, snow is white if and only if God says that snow is white. The real nature of things must be told to us by someone who actually knows it, since we cannot actually know it with our limitations. That is where the Word of God comes into play.

"We have an omniscient (all-knowing) God who has told us what is true. No other worldview is even capable, in their limited system, of being able to provide the 'ought' or the real nature of life. The Christian worldview is the only system that is even capable of the truth. Furthermore, the foundations on which we build at least demonstrate the capability of actually knowing what is really true. It is an 'all-knowing' God. On the contrary, the foundations of other non-theistic worldviews are not even capable of truth. Again, not capable. Not possible. There are many who would argue that our foundation, an 'all-knowing' God, has never been demonstrated to be true, whatever that means. However, my point is, our foundations, true or not, are capable of actual truth. Our God is the missing piece of Foundationalism (a philosophical theory concerning the justification of knowledge in the study of epistemology). Other views will fail because of man's limited abilities and all we have limitedly perceived and recorded. The best we could do is an educated guess, not what we could call truth. Remember, almost truth is not truth. There has not been a better solution from thousands of years of epistemic study. Jesus even clarified this when he asked the Father to sanctify the disciples with the truth and claimed that His Word is truth.

Make them holy by your truth; teach them your word, which is truth. (John 17:17)"

"I guess," Victoria said, "I now see why the reading and the preaching of the Word of God during church services is vitally important. I wonder, though, how many people actually see the Bible that way."

Daniel Taylor began to openly reflect with his family and Victoria on his study of world history. He remembered in the twenty-fist century the phenomena of what was referred to as *TED talks*. Hundreds of thousands of people would pay incredible amounts of money to hear speakers who were considered to be the top of their fields in technology, entertainment, and design. Many, of who the world would have considered part of the elite, would attend these conferences and hear the ideas decided to be, "worth spreading." He thought it amazing how billions would make it a point to hear the latest and greatest of these talks, yet, the doors were not coming off the hinges to hear the very Word of God that spoke the entire universe into existence and holds it all together. The things people will do for something like the *TED talks* but what they won't do for the Word of God, which is the truth.

"It is pretty sad when you think about it," Victoria said. "And yet, every Lord's Day, the Word of God is still being read in churches all over the world and the *TED talks* are done, filed away in the archives and completely obsolete today. The same Word that was ignored by so many over the years is still being publicly read, transforming and illuminating the lives of His people everywhere. Truly, heaven and earth will pass away, but His Word remains forever (Matthew 24:35)."

"Amen to that," Daniel said.

"So then, is it true that the reading of the Scriptures in church services and not just preaching have been something the church has been doing all this time?" Victoria asked.

"It has been then case since the Old Testament period," Daniel answered. "The Israelites under the direction of Moses did this as a common practice. It was the Law. (Deuteronomy 31:9-12) We also see reading the Word as a vital part of New Testament churches as well. For instance, Paul instructs Timothy for all churches to devote themselves to the public reading of the Scriptures (1 Timothy 4:13)."

Victoria added, "I guess maybe at times people, like me,"—she pointed to herself with the look of shame—"have somehow and some way lost confidence in the Word of God."

"It happens all the time," Michelle said. "That is why we go to church. We need to be reminded of the truth by the reading and preaching of the Word of Truth."

Daniel Taylor reached for his Bible and opened it up. "Nothing in this universe can compare to the Word of God. The Word of God created everything,
Then God said, "Let there be light," and there was light (Genesis1:3)
For when he spoke, the world began! It appeared at his command (Psalm 33:9)

"The Word of God even controls all things,
He sends his orders to the world— how swiftly his word flies! He sends the snow like white wool; he scatters frost upon the ground like ashes. He hurls the hail like stones. Who can stand against his freezing cold? Then, at his command, it all melts. He sends his winds, and the ice thaws (Psalm 147:15-18)

"We also see the wonderful persuasion of the Word of God,
"Let these false prophets tell their dreams, but let my true messengers faithfully proclaim my every word. There is a difference between straw and grain! Does not my word burn like fire?" says the LORD. "Is it not like a mighty hammer that smashes a rock to pieces? (Jeremiah 23:28-29)

"And, this one is my absolute favorite verse about the Word of God. The Word of God will accomplish what it intends to do,
"The rain and snow come down from the heavens and stay on the ground to water the earth. They cause the grain to grow, producing seed for the farmer and bread for the hungry. It is the same with my word. I send it out, and it always produces fruit. It will accomplish all I want it to, and it will prosper everywhere I send it (Isaiah 55:10-11)

"We also see in the New Testament a clear presentation that our Lord Jesus is the divine Logos. He is the manifestation of the Word of God and all things were made through Him. (John 1:3) We see here the clear greatness and power in the Word of God. This is why we want the Scriptures read to us as much as possible. It will transform us, hold us, and penetrate our very being,
For the word of God is alive and powerful. It is sharper

than the sharpest two-edged sword, cutting between soul and spirit, between joint and marrow. It exposes our innermost thoughts and desires (Hebrews 4:12)"

Daniel Taylor closed his Bible and rested it on the table next to his tray.

"Wow," Victoria said, with an encouraged smile. "I am truly excited and no longer confused. The Word of God is the truth and we can rest on His promises. I know that God has charge over my son and I know that His Word will accomplish all that He desires for Zach. I got it."

Michelle added. "Please know that we will keep you in our prayers."

Victoria nodded and smiled at Michelle. "Thank you both."

Daniel and his family along with Victoria disposed of the recyclables and headed toward the exit to get their retinal scans. As Victoria waited her turn, she looked back at the table where her son Zach was sitting and watched him laugh with his friends. She smiled and exhaled with a little giggle.

All together, they walked out through the doors as the wall to the right of the exit, displaying a digital projection scene of a sunny day on the beach, began to glitch continuously. This reminded everyone in *the Diner* that these are just images, and the reality of their underground existence wiped away the smiles.

6 PREACHING THE WORD PT. 1

Ethan Gold, the pastor of Salem Lutheran Church, stood in line with his wife for breakfast. When Ethan finished seminary, he was immediately installed as the pastor of Salem Lutheran after the passing of his predecessor from a heart attack induced by vitamin D deficiency. He and his wife, Olivia, have been in this call for the past 20 years and have been considered by many to be wonderful and loving shepherds in the underground congregation. Ethan is a competent theologian with good communication skills, yet it is said, that he can be a bit lackadaisical when it comes to disciplinary actions needing to be enforced on church members. He has shoulder length hair and a goatee, an obvious extrovert with dark green eyes.

The word around Salem is that Ethan Gold has had a major influence on the other pastors in Salem with regard to preaching. He has guided and directed the form and delivery of their sermons and has even had an influence on the great preaching of Dr. Daniel Taylor at Salem Presbyterian. Along with that, he has been able to get all the pastors in Salem to meet on a regular basis to talk, share ideas, and encourage one another in brotherly love. The pastors of Salem will all say that the other pastors in the community, are some of their best friends and it is clear in the eyes of the people of Salem. The Gold's cannot have children and have dedicated their time and efforts to each other and to the overall ministry in the underground.

As they moved closer to the service window, Landon Foster, walked up to the Gold's and smiled. Ethan and Olivia looked at everyone around the line embarrassed and wondering if the surrounding others were upset at Landon's cutting in. Landon noticed their discomfort.

"Don't you guys worry. I'm in Operations. I do not need to stand in line if I'm on duty."

Landon took off his badge from his jacket and held it up in the air and shouted, "Don't worry everyone. I am an Operations tech and I'm on duty. All is well. Just want to hang with some of my friends."

Everyone in Salem understands the importance of an Operations tech when he is on duty. It means that something in the structure of the facility is not working. It could be a serious problem or at least be such an irritant that the majority would want it fixed right away.

"So Landon, what-cha working on today?" Ethan asked.

"Well, the display on the wall at the entrance has been glitching since late last night. Had to shut down the whole system to troubleshoot. Wanted to get it fixed before breakfast, but to no avail. We're not

THE DINER: WHY IS CHURCH IMPORTANT?

going to have scenery for breakfast today. Oh well."

"I'm sure people will survive without it for at least one day," Ethan said.

"You would think so but my friend in Medical says that people suffer from many psychological problems when the scenery is down. That's why when the scenery is down, we get a code red in Operations and everyone has to report for duty."

"Wow," Ethan replied. "You know, after all this time, I didn't know that people had a difficult time when the scenery is down."

"Yeah, I still don't understand it though. So check this out. All the scenes are supposed to help us forget that we are underground, right?" Landon looked at the Gold's making sure they were in agreement. They both nodded. "Okay so the favorite scene of the people here, in Salem, is the beach scene. We get a shot of the ocean, the beach and some palm trees. Now this is the actual scene,"—he pointed his finger around *the* Diner—"all around us. Three-hundred and sixty degrees. So everywhere you look there is ocean all around. Somebody help me understand something. We don't like the feeling of being underground, but we like the feeling of being trapped on a small island?"

Ethan laughed. "You know, I never thought of it that way."

Landon Foster graduated top of his class in electrical engineering. He is a thoughtful, good-looking and relatively conceited young man with short blonde hair and brown eyes. He is smart, knows it, and wants everyone else to know it. He likes to sing everywhere he goes at work or at play. Consequently, all the other tech's in Operations call him *Gaston* after the character in the classic animated movie *Beauty and the Beast* by Disney. He is engaged to Christy Suzuki who also works as a tech in the Operations department. The Gold's and Landon sat at a table with their trays and Ethan asked the blessing over their meal. *This is the Diner. It is the Law. You need it. Your neighbor needs it.*

'So," Olivia said, "we got French toast and Canadian bacon today. I love how for breakfast we call it Canadian bacon and for lunch and dinner we call it ham. It's the same piece of meat."

Ethan and Landon laughed as they watched Olivia cut and eat the piece of meat.

"Well then, so other than fixing the scenery, what else is going on in your life? How is Christy?" Ethan asked.

"Christy is doing okay," Landon said, with the look of optimism. "She is working a lot lately in import and export."

"That's right. She works on the transports," Ethan said.

"Yeah, transportation has been very busy these days. Something about supplies running low in the other communities, especially Zion. You know how it goes, we gotta watch each others backs."

"We may need their help someday," Olivia said.

"That is very true," said Ethan.

"It gets hard after a while though," Landon said, with a frustration. "Sometimes it feels like we just keep failing. We just can't keep up with all that needs our attention. Its like, we fix something and before we can get caught up with the other things that need to be fixed, it breaks again. You know, it kinda feels like our job is just degrees of failure. We will never succeed. All we have is just good failure and bad failure." Landon put his head on the table.

Ethan and Olivia sat in wonder. They looked at each other, Ethan shrugged his shoulders, then they both looked at Landon.

"Um. Landon honey, are you okay?" Olivia asked.

Landon continued to talk as if he had never stopped. "Maybe you feel the same when preach on Sunday's concerning our sin and good works. We just cannot fulfill the perfect requirements that it takes to fulfill the Law of God no matter how hard we try. Its like degrees of failure. I can't remember, but you gave an example. Something about"—he put his hands up with shrugged shoulders and looked at Ethan to see if he was following—"grades in school or something like that."

"Yeah, I got it now." Ethan laughed. "When we start in on comparing our 'good works' with others and believe that we are really fulfilling the requirements of the Law since we are doing it better than others, we show we are blind to the truth of our real failure. We feel pretty good about our performance, but in reality, it's all a failure. Furthermore, we find that our pride, at times, brings us to the place of boasting in our 'righteous acts'. But in reality, we failed. We are like a group of students boasting over who got the better 'F' on the test. One got a twenty, one got a thirty five, one even got a fifty-nine. What difference does it make, they are all 'F's.'"

"Yeah," Landon said. "So let me ask you this. I know you have single handedly revolutionized the preaching here in Salem with this new paradigm. However, I am still wondering why it is that you feel the Gospel must be punctuated at the end of every sermon? Is it because of this view? Does it really have to be that way every Sunday?"

"Let me ask you this. Do you think that the Gospel is only for those who are not Christians?" Ethan asked.

"Well no," Landon replied, "I think it's good that we are reminded of the Gospel from time to time, but are we not supposed to move on to more maturity. Get off the milk and move on to solid food."

"Do you think that the Gospel isn't what brings us to maturity?"

"Well, I guess that is kinda the question. What is maturity to you, Mr. Ethan? Is it only the Gospel that can bring it?" Landon asked.

"A person who has grown in the grace and knowledge of our Lord Jesus (2 Peter 3:18) and in who, endurance is being developed. Endurance is increasing and we die more and more to sin and live more and more unto righteousness by faith. And all of this comes from a steady diet of the Gospel; hearing that Jesus came into this world to seek and save those who are lost. (Luke 19:10)"

"But like you just said," Landon firmly stated. "We are supposed to decrease sin and increase righteousness. In my mind, that means we need to stop sinning and do more good works. Now, you give us the Law and then the Gospel, but you don't tell us what we are supposed to do after that. What about what we are supposed to do?"

"That is a common question," Ethan said. "This is where preaching sometimes goes wrong. See, you already know what you are supposed to do. You just heard the Law preached. What you heard in the Law is what you are supposed to do. However, it does not take long till we find we are not successful in keeping that Law. That is why we need to hear the Gospel. We need to hear how we are forgiven for not keeping the Law like we should. With the Gospel, we hear of repentance, the forgiveness of sins and the victory we have, in Christ, who has done it all for our complete deliverance."

"Okay, I got that. But what are we supposed to do after we hear the Gospel and are now excited to do something good for God?" asked Landon.

"You do the Law that was addressed. That is what we are supposed to do."

"Yeah. But most likely, we will fail at it again. Right?"

"Probably."

"But wait. There has to be something else that we can actually do?" Landon asked, in desperation.

"What?" Ethan looked at Landon with his shoulders shrugged and hands up.

"You just set me up, didn't you." Landon had the look of defeat on his face. "Okay, explain."

"God has already told us what he wants us to do," Ethan answered. "It's called the Law. That's all I see in the Scriptures concerning His commands. However, I do see what it is you are reaching for. I know what you are wanting. You want me to give you an application where you will actually succeed. But what is the end game? Why do we want this? Pride? Self-worth? What?

"See. I knew you were setting me up." Landon leaned back chewing his food and held up his hand as if to say, "ok, you got my attention".

"Just a couple quick adjustments in your thinking.

What we tend to do as Christians, is the same thing that was done by the Pharisees. They interpreted the Law in such a way as to make it possible to keep. We think today that it must be understood that particular way. 'Why does God ask us to follow the Laws if he knows we can't do it? If we can't do it, He won't demand it. This understanding is wrong.

"For example, when we listen to sermons we want to hear something like the following: The Law is given, that we should meditate upon the Word of God day and night and after hearing, we realize how we fail at doing this. We are then broken and convicted. What we then hear, is the Gospel proclaimed of how Christ forgives us of the sin of not meditating upon the Word of God day and night. We feel gratitude for that wonderful gift and are now ready to be told what we are to do in light of the Gospel. You want the preacher to answer the question, 'so what now?' What are we supposed to do in light of the Gospel?

"Many times, what we are given, is a just try to read it a couple of times a week and God will be happy with that. Or God understands our weakness and if we meditate on his Word four to five times a week He will be pleased with us. Or God is happy with you as long as you are trying to read the Bible at all. Do that, and you will be ok. God does not really expect us to be able to actually fulfill the Law, so He is good as long as we try. As long as there is sincere effort and intension then we are pleasing to God. We get 'Low Law' so to speak. You with me?"

"I think so. Keep going," Landon said.

"Two things happen here. The first thing is that people fall under even more condemnation when they can't even do the lesser version of the Law. They don't meditate after the first day and live the rest of the week in utter condemnation because of their failure. They wrongly have their confidence in their ability not in Christ's complete work. Secondly, there are those that actually do the lighter work and think they are truly meeting the standard of God's Law and as a result, God is truly pleased with them and their efforts. Pride sets in, but it is actually based on a false belief. They also, have wrongly put their confidence in their abilities and not in the cross work of Christ. They have the belief that as long as they give some effort to this end Christ will make the effort perfect. However, we are not pleasing to God because our imperfect work was perfected by Christ. We are pleasing to God because we received credit for Christ's perfect work. We are not given credit for presenting a broken cup that was refurbished and made like new. We got credit for presenting the greatest and most perfect cup ever made. Do we think that God would or could settle for anything less? We are pleasing to God not because of the perfected work of a man, but because of the perfect work of the Son of Man."

"Ok, now you're losing me. This is really difficult to comprehend. It's pretty mind boggling." Landon laughed.

"Okay. Let's try it this way. We all have a tendency towards works righteousness. It is our very nature to want to accomplish things and receive rewards for the accomplishment. Even after we become Christians, we struggle with it. We want to be pleasing to God, we want to show him how good we are, we try to show him we are not a total loss, and we want to show God that he made a good decision when He chose us. Many believe that we become Christians because of grace, but we remain Christians by doing good works, and since we are the ones who can keep it, therefore, we need to keep it. As a result, we deceive ourselves when we do works and think that they are good when they are not. Or worse yet, in thinking that these imperfect and tainted works of ours would actually be acceptable to a Holy God. The work of salvation did not lower God's standards of righteousness for Christians in that God now gives us a break or is now more lenient in the standards expected of us. In actuality, the work of salvation is the giving of credit for actually doing the work at the high standard required of a Holy God. His standard was not lowered. It was met. It was met by us, because the work of Christ was credited to us.

"We have, at times, forgotten this. We assert that we are the people of God and therefore we are supposed to really keep the Law. And, like the Pharisees, we tend to deceive ourselves. We think we are following God's Law, but we are really keeping the imperfect law of man."

"Right," said Landon. "You said that this kind of thinking is like the Pharisees."

"The Pharisees had interpreted the Laws in such a way that it lessened the true requirements and gave them the illusion they were really keeping it. This is why they didn't see the need to be saved from their sin. They were righteous in their eyes and did not see their need for salvation from sin. Furthermore, it caused them to believe that they did not need to be freed from the bondage of sin, but believed they needed salvation from the oppression of the Romans.

They then rejected the Messiah and His Gospel wrongly. In addition, Jesus made it very clear in the Sermon on the Mount that many of the current interpretations and understandings of the Law were not correct (Matthew 5-7). They missed the true purpose of the Law.

"In essence, Jesus described the understanding of the Pharisees concerning anger as not upholding the reality of what the Law demands. Sure, if you murder your neighbor, you will be judged, but Christ also asserts that if you are angry with your neighbor you will also be subject to the same judgment. It is not just a sin when taking the life of a person, it is also sin if you are angry with, or even insult, another person.

"Sure, it is a sin if you commit adultery, however, it is also a sin if you look lustfully upon a women because you have committed adultery with her in your heart. The Law is not just about the actual action of the sin, but also, what's in the person's heart. The Pharisees were very concerned about their external actions, but Christ is demonstrating how what is happening inside of us is also an important concern.

"It is not just the action, but also the disposition of a person's heart. When we see this addition of Christ's teaching, it brings us to the tremendous reality of our sin. We realize how deep sin really goes and how far we really are from God and His Law. Sadly, I am sinning against God with even a split second of something not right in my mind and heart. To make matters worse, James says in chapter two,

For the person who keeps all of the laws except one is as guilty as a person who has broken all of God's laws (James 2:10).

"The reality of it all is that we need to see how far

short we actually come in keeping the Law of God and come to the realization that our problem is not the Romans, food and water, relationships, sickness, poverty, or suffering. Our problem is the Wrath of God. This is the judgment that comes from the breaking of His commands and not rightly keeping his Law. This is the true purpose of the Law. The Law was not given on Mount Sinai to be kept as the original requirements of the Covenant of Works since that Covenant was already broken. It was given to show us that we are utterly sinful and we need salvation (Romans 7:7)."

"Is that how we understand sin? Breaking the Law?" Landon asked.

"Basically." Ethan nodded his head. "More specifically, I would define it as not complying with the Law of God and breaking the Law of God. Even more specifically, sin is both, not doing what God commands and doing what God forbids."

"Wow," said Landon. "And there are lots of Laws to ignore and break."

"Yes sir."

"Okay but," Landon said, "didn't Jesus make things easier when He summarized the whole Law for us? You know, cutting it down to two. When he told us to love God and love our neighbor he showed that the whole Law hangs on these two commands. All we have to do, technically, is follow these two commands. He made things way easier for us. Right?"

"Yes, He sure did," Ethan answered.

As Ethan sat back in his chair with a smile on his face, Landon felt like he was just set up, again.

"So Jesus did make it easier for us to keep the

Law."

"No."

"I knew it, you set me up again."

Ethan said, "I agreed that Jesus made things easier for us when he summarized the whole Law with the Great Commandment. However, I did not specify what he actually made easier."

"That's true." Landon laughed.

"It is not now, easier to keep. But if we are truly honest with ourselves and have a clear understanding of what the Law requires, then we would realize that he made it easier for us to see we do not keep the commandments."

Other people sitting near the conversation listened in on the exchange between Landon and Ethan. One person even turned his chair around.

"Ah. Got it. But I'm pretty sure that I loved God and my neighbor this week."

"Honestly?" Ethan asked.

"Nah. I was just messing with you. You made a good point. If we are honest, it really is easier to see our failure."

Landon sat back and thought as he continued to eat his French toast.

Ethan continued, "Think about it. It says in John, *Do not love this world nor the things it offers you, for when you love the world, you do not have the love of the Father in you. For the world offers only a craving for physical pleasure, a craving for everything we see, and pride in our achievements and possessions. These are not from the Father, but are from this world (1 John 2:15-16).*

"Have we love for the world? If there is, then there is no room for the love of the Father in that person. You cannot love the world and the Father at the same time."

"Why is this not possible?" asked Landon.

"Jesus said it Himself,
No one can serve two masters. Either he will hate the one and love the other, or he will be devoted to the one and despise the other. You cannot serve both God and Money (Matthew 6:24)."

"I see," Landon said. "I guess when you see it from that direction, it becomes evident that there were several times last week when I was not very loving to God."

"And what of your neighbor?" asked Ethan.

"Well, maybe. I don't think I did anything bad to anyone this week. Yeah, I followed the 'Golden Rule.'"

"Okay, you did not do anything bad, but did you do anything good?" Ethan asked.

"Hmm. I guess I don't know. Why does that matter?"

"Basically, that is the essence of the 'Golden Rule', given by Jesus. Other belief systems and teachers of religion and philosophy have their own version of the 'Golden Rule;' made up of, essentially, refraining from doing bad things to people. In substance, don't do to others what you would not want done to you. On the other hand, Jesus says, 'Do to others whatever you would like them to do to you.' This is the essence of all that is taught in the Law and the prophets (Matthew 7:12). The other 'Golden Rules' deal with refraining from doing bad things, but Jesus' rule is concerned with doing good things to your neighbor. It is simply not enough to keep from doing wrong to your neighbor, you also need to do good things for them. Do the things you wish someone would do for you if you were in their shoes. If you did not do this, then you did not love your neighbor. This is the very nature of the Law of God."

More people around the table, where Ethan and Landon were having their conversation, listened in, and got Olivia's attention.

"Okay then. I see how that changes everything. But what about now?" Landon asked. "We already saw our sinfulness and realized that we needed a Savior. That is why we are Christians today. But what now? What about works now? Are we not saved unto good works?"

The entire conversational volume lowered as people sitting near Landon and the Gold's seemed to nod their head in approval of Landon's question.

"Yes we are and as Christians, we will see the fruits of thankfulness. Nevertheless, we should understand something about good works and the part it plays in the life of a Christian."

"Okay. Hit the brakes." Landon put his hands up as if he were attempting to stop a moving vehicle.

Just then, and man named Jordan walked up to the table and said, "May I join you all? This is a really interesting conversation."

"Sure," Olivia said, with a smile. "Have a seat."

"May I join you as well?" Shirley, another person sitting at a table near Ethan and Landon asked.

"Please join us. You are all welcome to join us," Olivia said, with a loud voice. She was attempting to let everyone listening in to the conversation to join in, if they wanted too.

"Okay. First of all, what are good works?" Landon asked

"It is only the works that are founded on true faith and are in strict accordance with the very Law of God. If the work is from our own imagination, something instituted by man, or not from faith, then it is not a good work. Clearly, it must be founded on faith, and this part is the biggy. Hebrews 11:6 makes it clear that it is impossible to please God without faith. Therefore, it does not even matter how perfect the action is, no faith, no way."

Landon and the others nodded their heads in understanding.

Ethan continued, "What is acceptable to God is the perfectly good and compete work of Christ. Consequentially, we become acceptable to God because the perfectly good work of Christ has been given to us and applied to us by the Spirit. This can only be so, by no other way, than by faith.

"Additionally, the work also has to be in exhaustive accordance to the Law of God, not what we imagined we accomplished, nor what was in accordance with the directives of another person. It really has to be in line with what God commanded."

"See. But that is the problem," Landon replied. "If it is to be in line with what God actually demands, then we will never be able to do it. What our Holy God wants, is a work that is absolutely perfect and pure. We could never do this because our works will always be imperfect and tainted with sin like you said."

"You got it," Ethan answered. "We need to understand that the distance between our best works and the perfection of what our Holy God requires is larger than we can imagine. Again, no matter how well you do, we will always come up short. Always.

THE DINER: WHY IS CHURCH IMPORTANT?

"Four men were standing before the Grand Canyon. They were talking about how far it was to the other side of the canyon when an argument broke out between the three of them about who was the better jumper. One claimed to be a record holder for the long jump. One claimed to be able to dunk a basketball. One claimed to be able to jump over a moving vehicle. The conversation got heated as they continued to debate over who could jump the farthest across. Finally, the man who was not a part of the argument piped in and said, 'You know what guys, who cares. If you guys jump, no matter who goes the farthest, you are all going to die.' No matter who is actually closer to fulfilling the Law, even if it is better than others, it will not matter. If we don't do it perfectly, then we didn't do it at all."

Landon said, "I see, but you are making,"—he moved his chair over to make more room for more people joining them—"making it seem like it is impossible to be obedient. If we can't fulfill the Law why does God still want our imperfect obedience?"

"We need it and our neighbor needs it," Ethan answered. "First of all, our obedience serves as a testimony, to others, of our gratitude for the blessings he has given us. God is truly praised and glorified by us as we thank Him for His wonderful blessings, which will, in turn, be witnessed by others. Others, will see our grateful obedience to that end, which is the end they reject, and will serve as a testimony of the wonderful salvation we have received to the glory of our Lord.

"Secondly, we and others, in light of our grateful obedience, can be assured of our union with Christ, seeing the fruits of our faith. Remember, however, we do not bring forth the fruit, God does. We may water and care for the tree, but it is God who brings the fruit. Furthermore, let us also not forget that God can bring forth fruit even if there is no one to water or care for the tree. Therefore, the fruit that you bear is not assurance, to you and others, as by-product of your efforts and abilities. The fruit is assurance, to you and to others, that the Spirit of God lives in you. And because He lives in you, you bear fruit. It is the fruit of the Spirit (Galatians 5:22-23). When we are in doubt of our salvation, it is not, 'I know I'm a Christian because look at what I have done for God. But it's 'I know I am a Christian because look at what He has done in me.'

"Finally, our obedience serves to bring others to Christ. Martin Luther, our beloved reformer, said, 'God does not need your good works, but your neighbor does.' Therein lies the problem. Many of us believe that it is our obedience and good works that will keep us in God's good graces causing us to believe that God's love for us is dependent on what we do and not on what Christ has done. Understand, we cannot have the attitude of now I have to pay God back for what he has done for us. As Christians, who are justified, everything between us and God are already settled by the work of Christ, forever. His work is perfect, one-hundred percent. We cannot add to it, nor take from it. To believe that we can add to it or take from it, is essentially unbelief in God's Word. If we were to do 'good works' to this end, our first step in this direction is a sin and not a good work at all, because the motive is unbelief. Therefore, God's acceptance of us, because of the perfect work of Christ, can't be added to nor taken away. He does not need them, but your neighbor needs you to obey God's command to preach the Gospel to the ends of the earth. They need to hear the Gospel so they can believe. Our neighbor needs our good works."

Both, Shirley and Jordan, had tears fall from their faces as Ethan finished his explanation. Even more people pulled their chairs around the table.

"Tell me then, what about all promises of reward?" Landon asked.

"Yes we will be rewarded," Ethan answered. "But, it will be because of grace not because of our works. Nothing we do will ever obligate God to give us anything. The reward that He has promised to us is not because of a debt He now owes us, but because it is something he wants to give us. Because of his grace, the unmerited favor He has for His people, we will receive a reward. Think about it. Jesus gave us the parable,

"When a servant comes in from plowing or taking care of sheep, does his master say, 'Come in and eat with me'? No, he says, 'Prepare my meal, put on your apron, and serve me while I eat. Then you can eat later.' And does the master thank the servant for doing what he was told to do? Of course not. In the same way, when you obey me you should say, 'We are unworthy servants who have simply done our duty.'" (Luke 17:7-10)

"You see. He owes us nothing. Even if we did or even could do everything He has asked or commanded, it would still amount to nothing. We only did our duty. He will never owe us anything, never owe us a 'thank you'. Therefore, the reason we receive anything or more specifically, any reward, is just because of the grace of our Lord. Moreover, the only reason we have anything at all to do with God is because He decided to have something to do with us in the first place. The technical theological term is, 'condescension'. This is His wonderful grace. The grace that is sufficient for us and the grace by which we stand."

"Okay. But it seems that the Scriptures shows degrees of reward in accordance to what we do here and now? The more good works we do on earth, the more reward we get in heaven. More crowns, bigger mansion, more jewels, and more rank in heaven. Maybe?"

"Good question," Ethan said. "Now we can't look at all of the Scriptures like this now, but we could say that they are generally causing us to look to heaven for your reward, not to rewards on earth. Being rewarded according to what we have done does not necessarily imply degrees of reward in heaven. We should also remember that the word 'reward' is also used in a negative sense. For those who rebel against God the Scriptures declare that they will receive their just reward (Isaiah 3:11) and this reward is the wrath of God. It is payment according to what they have done. So in these instances of Scripture, we could see that the contrast is between the reward of heaven and the reward of condemnation, and not between a big reward in heaven and a little reward in heaven.

"However, more importantly. If you ask me if there are degrees of reward in heaven I should say no. The Scriptures state,

LORD, you alone are my inheritance, my cup of blessing. You guard all that is mine. (Psalm 16:5)

"Christ alone is our inheritance, or in other words,

our reward. Can there be anything better than Christ alone?"

"I'm guessing I'm supposed to say no." Landon laughs

"Good answer," Ethan said with a smile on his face. "Now in Christ is all we could ever need. In Christ alone is more than we could ever ask or imagine. His riches are unsearchable and His blessing are overflowing. How in the world could anything be added to Him that will make us feel like we got more? No matter what you may add to Christ it will never make the deal sweeter. He is all that there is, and He is the most complete and all encompassing reward that could ever be given. We will need nothing more, nor desire anything more. How in the world could we ever think that if all we got is Christ that we would feel like it is even possible to have anymore? How could we ever feel like someone would have it better if they had more than Christ? No matter what we are given, nothing will ever come close to Christ alone. The Scriptures declare,

Whenever the living beings give glory and honor and thanks to the one sitting on the throne (the one who lives forever and ever), the twenty-four elders fall down and worship the one sitting on the throne (the one who lives forever and ever). And they lay their crowns before the throne and say, "You are worthy, O Lord our God, to receive glory and honor and power. For you created all things, and they exist because you created what you pleased." (Revelation 4:9-11)

"When we are with Christ there will be nothing we could be given that we will not want to throw down at His feet. Nothing else will come close to bringing us more joy and satisfaction than Christ and Christ alone. He alone will be all we desire, and there can be nothing more. That is our awesome Lord, Christ Jesus. Whew, I'm ready to preach, I got so excited!

7 PREACHING THE WORD PT. 2

"Alright,"—he held his hands up—"easy there partner," Landon said with a smile. "More questions please. When you say all of this, it almost makes me feel like we can just be carefree and irresponsible and it is all okay. It does not matter, so I can just live life doing whatever I want to do. It does not matter."

"Ah, yes indeed," Ethan responded. "But it's not possible for a person who has true faith and love for Christ to live a life that way. If you are really a Christian there will be fruits of thankfulness, repentance, and worship because of the Spirit living in you. John Bunyan, the author of *Pilgrims Progress*, was in prison and befriended by many who were with him. Some of them were Anabaptists. They did not appreciate how Bunyan preached the Gospel, especially, that which concerns the love of God. Dr. Bryan Chapell, of the twenty-first century, wrote in his book *Holiness by Grace* of a particular encounter, 'If you keep assuring the people of God's love,' the opponents argued, 'they will do whatever they want.'

Replied Bunyan, 'If I assure God's people of His love, then they will do whatever He wants.' Another way of looking at it, Landon. Would you agree that not everything that sparkles is a diamond?"

"Yes I would"

"And, every diamond sparkles."

"Yes"

"Therefore, not every 'work' is done by a Christian, but every Christian will 'work.'"

"Wow," Landon said. "Ok, that really brought it all together for me."

Many of the people that joined in on the conversation nodded with Landon as he finished making his statement.

Ethan said, "James chapter two makes all of this very clear."

"Right, okay. So then why the warning? Why the rebuke?"

"Warning passages and those spurring them on to good works are what is needed by Christians who are being deceived, have lost their way or have become complacent and apathetic in their life. Only Christians will truly heed the warnings of the Scriptures. Even if an unbeliever heeds the warnings to do good works, it would fall into the realm of works righteousness and he will still be condemned. If I was hiking with my son and he got close to the edge and I was on a different level, I would shout a warning to him. If he keeps walking, he will fall over the edge. When I warn him, tell him to stop and turn around, because he is my son and he trusts me, he will heed my warning and will be safe. Believers will heed the warnings of the Scriptures because we trust Christ and through faith, we will be safe from the consequences.

"Furthermore, a person who does not have trust in me, if I were to shout a warning to them, they may not listen to my warnings. A person who does not like me and wants nothing to do with me will probably not heed my warnings. This is why unbelievers will probably not heed the warnings of God. In hindsight, this is the way it has been since the beginning. Remember, the people before the great flood in Genesis were warned by Enoch and Noah, yet they did not listen. Warnings and rebukes in the Scriptures are for the guidance, discipline, and edification of Christians. Additionally, the warnings serve as all the more reason for the condemnation of unbelievers. Consequently, they will be judged and yet, it will be much worse, because they were warned."

"More specifically," Landon asked. "What about James chapter two? Faith without works is dead. We as Christians need to have works. That is the point."

"Yes." Ethan noticed people now sitting on the floor around the table with trays in their hands. He wondered if the Holy Spirit was now doing a work in *the Diner*. "But, again, the works we do are the result of being born again. Our works are showing that we really do have true faith in Christ because of the fruit that the Spirit brings in and from us. James desired the Christian's to whom he was writing, to awaken out of their slumber, apathy and laziness, to become aware of the deception leading them away from the truth, and to spur them on to more endurance and maturity. It is probable he is dealing with those who have adopted an erroneous view called 'Antinomianism.' They are simply those who don't believe that the Law of God has anything to do with a Christian anymore. The Law does not even serve as a guide for the believer; therefore, there is no more need to do any works in accordance to the Law of God.

"Nevertheless, he wanted to encourage them with the understanding that a faith that does not have works, is not true saving faith. Is it true faith, to simply say that you have it? Just saying that you believe does not mean that you truly do believe. What we need to be aware of, to make sure we understand this principle, is to be clear on what it is that James is declaring. If the person has no works, then his faith is dead. Period. This biblical truth will awaken the Christian and expose the real state of an anti-nomian or unbeliever. If there is no works then the person might not be a Christian.

"Now, if they are truly a Christian, they will be awakened from their apathy, be redirected away from their deception and progress to good works motivated by the love they have for God. If they really are an unbeliever then the pressure for good works will be an instruction in works righteousness. Essentially, we would be telling them do good works if you want to be a Christian. This cannot be the case. This would surely be false teaching of the worst kind. Understand, if a person really has no works then he may really be an unbeliever. What they need is the Gospel, not the exhortation to do more works. Vital to our understanding of this passage of Scripture is knowing that James is not claiming a justification of being right with God, but a justification for the existence of true faith. Paul used the example of Abraham to show faith as the instrument by which we become right with God and James used the example of Abraham to confirm that Abraham really had faith. Paul shows justification by faith and James shows justification of faith. Paul showed Abraham was righteous because of faith and James shows that Abraham faith was,"—he pumped his fist—"righteous." Ethan laughed.

"James warned them. If they are Christians they will follow. They will realize what is happening and react accordingly. They realize that they are not being who they are. They will not move to works to demonstrate that they are a child of God, they will move to works because they are a child of God. It's like Aristotle's virtue ethics. Are the virtues good because they are good themselves or are they good because good people do them? Essentially, virtues are the things that good people do. Even though lying may be wrong generally, if a good person were to lie, it will be virtuous to lie at that particular time. All conclusions are based on the character of the person than the actions themselves. Now remember, I use this view of Aristotle's as a different vantage point for explanation, not as our actual framework for ethics. Our ethical framework is always the Bible.

"In our case, are the good works good because they are good or are the good works good because people of faith do them? No matter how good the work, without faith it is impossible to please Him. Therefore, only the people of true faith can do good works and they are moved because they have true faith. Unbelievers may do the same kind of work, but because there is no genuine faith, it can never be a good work. Consequently, we do not demonstrate that we are Christians by our works, but only by our faith in the promises of God. The genuineness of our faith is confirmed by our works. Very important distinction."

"I don't see why the distinction is important," Landon said. "It almost feels like it does not matter."

"I understand, but the distinction maybe in a sense be so closely tied that they feel like they are one and the same, but the distinction is necessary if the proposition is reversed. In dealing with propositional knowledge, namely, necessary and sufficient conditions, structuring the right to left and the left to right direction of the proposition is required. Bear with me here. If X knows P, then X and P have features F1, F2, F3, ect. We also need to be able to say, if X and P have features F1, F2, F3, ect., then X knows P. Therefore, our works cannot demonstrated that we are Christians. If I know that you are a Christian then I have intimate knowledge that you have faith in Christ and you have faith in Christ. If I have intimate knowledge that you have faith in Christ and you have faith in Christ, then I know you are a Christian. Great! But what if I say, If I know you are a Christian then I have intimate knowledge that you do works and you do works. If I have intimate knowledge that you do works and you do works, then I know that you are a Christian. Does that work?"

"No. It is possible to do works and not be a Christian. Works cannot confirm our salvation so you cannot say that you know I am a Christian."

"Right. But if I know you have faith and you do have faith, then it is correct to say that you are a Christian. Yes?"

"Yes."

"Let me also, put it this way. If I ask you how do

THE DINER: WHY IS CHURCH IMPORTANT?

you know you are a Christian, what would you say?"

"Because I have faith in Christ."

"Good answer. That is how our Christianity is demonstrated. Now, if I doubt the genuineness of your faith and ask, how do you know your faith is real?"

"Because of the good works that I do, empowered by the Spirit, discloses what I really believe."

"Nice job. You were listening." Ethan laughed. "You answered correctly because you can see the distinction in the propositions and when you go right to left or reverse it, the answers are still acceptable. If you did not see the distinction and believe that our Christianity is demonstrated by works, at least in part, then when you reverse it, we would conclude that we know that we are Christians by the works that we do. This is not correct. We are not Christians because of what we do, but because of what we believe. James cannot be asserting that our works provide the proof of our justification, because we are not saved by works. James is showing that works displays the reality of true faith in Christ. Our works display what we really believe."

"Now going back to James and his warnings. On the other hand, if they are not Christians then they will not follow the warnings given. They will truly have no works because they have no faith; their faith is dead and they really do not trust in Christ. Even though they say they have faith, their fruit is showing that they really do not have faith; therefore, the Spirit is not in them. How then can they do good works? They have to have living faith. How do they get living faith? Not by encouraging them to do more works, but by their hearing the Gospel preached.

That is why I hold a primacy on the preaching of the Gospel and ending with it. It is and has to be our only motivation to good works. The thing that causes us to move for the Lord is the message of the Lord. His wonderful Gospel."

"Hmm. Ok so I am almost there," Landon said. "I think you have just touched on a final problem. Why can't the Law of God be the thing that motivates us. Did you not say that James' exhortation, in a sense, motivates Christians. So, why can't that be the final point of exhortation in a sermon?"

"Great question, Landon. Okay, first of all, the reason for wanting to keep the Law is of vital importance. It cannot only be about the very actions of keeping the Law. Our motivations for doing so are foundational. For instance, if we desire to keep the Law so that we can gain favor or prove to Christ that we are worth keeping, then essentially, the motivation is unbelief and, therefore, sin. Or, if we are keeping the Law so that God will let us into heaven or put Him in our debt, then essentially, the motivation is unbelief and, therefore, sin. If we strive to be honest, but we are doing it because we are to be better than those who lie, saying or thinking, 'we are better than that', then our motive is, essentially sinful because of unbelief. Even if we are really passionate and sincere about it. Paul says in Romans concerning the Jews,

I know what enthusiasm they have for God, but it is misdirected zeal. For they don't understand God's way of making people right with himself. Refusing to accept God's way, they cling to their own way of getting right with God by trying to keep the law. (Romans 10:2-3)

"As Christians, we do not follow the Law to bring

us favor with God, to show him we are better than others, to try to pay Him back for His grace, or to ensure that we don't lose our salvation. We do not follow the Laws and commands of God in order to remain Christians, we follow the Laws because we are Christians. I do not have to act in such a way to prove to my dad and to myself that I am his son. To do that would be an act of mistrust of my father who said I was his son and ultimately hurtful to him. I love my dad and I trust that I am his son. I don't act like it. I just am. All the work I do for my dad is out of love for him, not because I have to prove to him that I am his son. Do you all see how twisted we can be to our heavenly Father? The fact we desire to follow the Laws, for no other reason than love for God, is the assurance we have faith in Christ. Our desire to obey purely out of love assures us we have faith and faith assures us we are Christians who are children of God. This distinction directs our motives and as we can see, motive is vital."

"Okay, however, we are at times obeying the Law," Landon said. "Why is that even a problem? If we are praying, then we are praying. God desires that we pray, what difference does motive really make?"

Ethan said, "Proverbs 28:9 says,
God detests the prayers of a person who ignores the law.

"Motive makes a huge difference. The only way we will really obey the Law is for it to be motivated by our love for God who first loved us. Just because we know it is a demand of God for us not to steal, it does not mean we won't steal. The Law tells us that God wants us not to covet, but it does not mean we won't covet. The Law tells us what is right but, that does not mean we are going to do it.

"A philosopher by the name David Hume, asserts that reason and knowledge do not motivate us to action. What motivates us is our passions and desires. I know that if I'm going to pass my upcoming test, I need to study. But that does not mean I'm going to. I know that if I want a bigger and better body, I need to work out. But that does not mean I'm going to. I know that it is rational, that if I want to be healthy and live, I need to eat here at *the Diner*. But that does not mean I'm going to. What motivates me to study is not knowing that to pass the test I have to study, but my desire to pass the test. What motivates me to work out is not knowing that to get a better body I have to work out, but my passion for a better body. What motivates me to eat at *the Diner* is not knowing I need to eat at *the Diner* to survive, but my desire to be healthy and survive.

"Knowledge and reason do not motivate, our desires do. In essence, we do what we want. We will not to do it, if we don't want to do it or if we would rather do something else. I know that if I do not empty my trash receptacle on disposal days, my home will overflow with trash. I know this, but it does not mean I will dispose of it. I may be caught up in a good book or watching a movie and decide I would rather do that, then take out the trash. Even though I know that I will regret it later. At that particular moment, I preferred to read the book than to dispose of the trash. It was my passion, my desire that motivated me. You may ask, why is this important?"

Landon and many of the people listening to Ethan speak nodded their heads in affirmation. Many of them have heard nothing like this before. At this time, it looked like a quarter of the Diner have

THE DINER: WHY IS CHURCH IMPORTANT?

gathered around Ethan, Olivia, and Landon to listen in.

Ethan continued, "It is essentially the same thing when it comes to obeying the Law of God. We know, through God's commands, what right and wrong actions are. But, just because we know that stealing is wrong, that does not mean we won't steal. We know that murder is wrong, but that does not mean we won't murder. The reason we don't steal is not because we know that it is wrong to steal, but because we don't want to steal. The reason we don't murder is not because we know it is wrong to murder, but because we don't want to murder.

"There is more to obedience than just knowing the Law, we need to want to obey the Law. We need to desire above all things, obedience to the Law. Furthermore, this is the reason we needed to be given a new heart, by God, when we became a Christian. It's why we needed to be born again to see the kingdom. It's why we needed the breath of life so we could have faith. We were so corrupted by sin we needed a whole new heart, not just a healed one. We should always remember that Christ did not come to make good people better, but He came to bring dead people back to life. We were by nature prone to hate God and our neighbor. Consequently, Christ needed to give us the life to want to love Him and the desire to serve him. The Law tells us what we are to do, but it does not motivate us to do it. Sure the fear of the consequences of not obeying the Law may motivate, but it is not because we know the Law. It is still based on what we desire. In order for us to truly walk in holiness, we have to desire to walk in true holiness. It cannot be any less.

"This is why I say you can preach the Law all you want, but it is not the knowing of the Law that will motivate good works, it has to be a change of heart. Many pastors of the past tried to motivate their people to obey the Laws of God by either fear or manipulation. They scared the people into good works by saying that if they don't do them, they will lose their salvation and go to hell or say that God will punish them in His wrath. In addition, they may try to sweeten the deal and say that if they obey the Laws, God will be pleased with them and reward them because of their efforts.

"These are things that motivate, but they will both, lead to hatred of God, eventually. Some will realize that everything bad in their lives is because they are being punished by God, instead of seeing it all as the actual effects of sin in this world. They will soon despair and eventually despise God. All of this is based on unbelief in God's promise that there is no condemnation for those who are in Christ and that once He has us in the palm of his hand, He will never let us go. All of that effort without knowing that the first step was already a failure.

"On the other hand, those who work and work to do well will come to realize that their life is not better, but may even be worse, will conclude that there is no reward and God is a liar. They will soon despair and eventually hate God. All of that effort without knowing that the very first step was already a failure because of unbelief.

"At its core, ultimately, these two reasons used to motivate people are flat lies. They are not true. Christians will not face the wrath of God in punishment. Jesus already bore it. Christians do not receive a reward for their efforts, but a reward by grace only. Our treasure is in heaven. All of our motivation must be founded by love for Him and our neighbor. It cannot be fear, reward, earning favor, comfort, money, or pride. Because of unbelief, we perceive God to be more like an employer than a Father. If we don't do our job, then we will get fired. He is not our employer, He declared that He is our Father. Fathers do not fire their sons for disobedience, they discipline them. Our disobedience will bring God's discipline, not His condemnation. Do we believe it? It must be love. All the commandments are summed up in, here's the key word, 'loving' God with all our heart, soul, mind, and strength and 'love' our neighbor as ourselves."

Landon replied, "It seems as if we are only interested in knowing what we are to do. We see good works as a means to an end. We cannot just do good works simply because it is good. We use it to gain something. That's why we only want to know what to do when in actuality, the important thing is how we can do it. Sound good?"

"Sounds very good," Ethan answered. "We know what to do for the most part already. Romans chapter two makes clear that even those without the Word of God still do what is required because the Law is written on our hearts. We know the Law naturally, what is foreign to us, is the Gospel. When we hear the Law, we find out what is good, but what we do not realize is that we do not have the ability in our own strength to do it. Therefore, the Law tells us what God wants us to do, and it is the Gospel that tells us how we can do it. If I am told that to live the good life I need to get upside, I know where I need to go for the good life. However, what is just as important is how I will actually get there. We know what is right. Do we know how to do it?"

"Yes!" Landon exclaimed. "I think I am understanding it now. That is why you all preach the Gospel and end with it every week. That is why you say that the same message that brought you to Christ is the same message that will keep you in Christ. It is the Gospel that brings the power of God for salvation. The power of Christ is how."

"Very good," Ethan said.

"Okay, so I lied," said Landon. "I have another question. So, is it then possible to live a holy life?"

"Absolutely. It is what God has called us to (2 Timothy 1:9). A Puritan long ago named, Walter Marshall, gave us four things you must receive from God, before you can live a godly life. This understanding has truly transformed my life.

"Number one, you have to want to obey God more than anything else. I demonstrated this point to you all already, but we need to be driven by love for God. If we really don't want to obey then we will fail. We cannot just look at obedience as pure duty. Like a sick person with medicine. We take it cause we have to, but hate every moment of it. Like a child with vegetables. They eat it cause they have to, but hate every minute of it. We can do them, but it is not true obedience. We have to love it. If we are to love God with all of our heart, then we will love his Law and love to obey Him. (John 14:23) This is difficult. We can't just flip a switch and start loving God. It is a work that God has to do and He has promised us He will. Remember, our 'flesh'. We are prone by nature to hate God and our neighbor. The Gospel is what we need to hear to bring a desire to love and obey God. (1 John 4:19)

"Number two, we have to be completely certain we are reconciled to God and that he truly accepts us. This is why we cannot depend on our works for assurance of salvation. We have to have assurance of salvation in order to have good works. We may have works, but they may be done in the sense of servile duty. This is not works motivated by love. We love because He first loved us. We need to be confident we are in right standing and accepted by God before we will truly obey. Furthermore, we cannot truly obey if we still think that we are going to hell, if it is still a possibility, or God is still our enemy and hates us. If we try to obey because we are afraid of condemnation then our obedience would be one of unbelief in God's Word. This is not obedience. There is no condemnation for those who are in Christ. How can we have faith in God's loving kindness if we believe that there is still a possibility of condemnation? How does it look to see God in His Word doing all He can to assure us of our wonderful future, but we cannot be assured? It is called unbelief. This is sin. Again, it is the Gospel that will give us that wonderful assurance.

"Number three, we have to also be confident that our future life will be happy and wonderful, with Christ, for eternity. The godly life is not possible if we don't think there is a wonderful afterlife. What is all of this for? If there is no wonderful afterlife, then why in the world would I choose suffering for Christ over pleasure? Why would we still be joyful, if people took everything from us and if we did not have a lasting inheritance in heaven? (Hebrews 10:34) Even

Paul said if there is no resurrection there is no hope, preaching is useless, faith is useless, we are still in our sins. If this is the case, then let us eat, drink and be merry for tomorrow we die (1 Corinthians 15:32). And, don't forget that Paul also said that if we have hope in this life only, then we are most to be pitied (1 Corinthians 15:19). If we are doubting and thinking that all of this is false, that we do not have a future to look forward too, then we will resign ourselves to apathy, because 'what's the point?' Even if we do works in this state, we are doing it in unbelief and it is impossible to please God in unbelief (Hebrews 11:6). It is the Gospel that increases our faith and enlightens us to the reality, wonder and beauty of our future eternity with our Lord.

"Number four, we need to be confident that God will cause us to desire and do what is His good pleasure. Many of us continue to think that obedience to God is like a light switch. We flip it on to obey and flip it off to disobey. We may find we are disobeying God and then because of conviction, we believe we can just flip the switch to stop, so we flip it. Here is the problem though. If it were really like that, then there would be no disobedience at all, simply because we would never turn it off. We cannot obey by our own will-power, God needs to give it to us. He will empower us to will and do of His good pleasure. (Philippians 2:13) As we have seen true obedience is not an easy thing. We saw that it is impossible on our own. Even Paul recognized this when he said that he labors and struggles with 'God's energy' working in him. (Colossians 1:29) A holy life must be one that is graciously given to us by God and God alone. It is truly a good work because it is His perfect work. His work, is not tainted with sin and imperfect."

"So, can we actually do good works? Is it even possible?"

"Yes, because it is His work in us, not ours. If it is actually done, it will be by the hand of Christ. Again, His work in us, not our work for Him. Our work for Him is imperfect and His work in us is perfect. It is clear, we will walk the godly life only by His means, not by ours, for He will not share His glory with anyone. His means, all of which is given to us by grace and received by faith. And where do we get this truth? From the Gospel."

"Now I understand why the Gospel is primary in the sermon," Landon said. "Everything in our life begins, continues, and ends with the Gospel. The Gospel is everything. Everything in and out of our life is in Christ and in Christ alone. Our holiness and godliness comes from God and we must be confident, in faith, that He will give the power He promised. We know where to go, we lack the power to get there."

"Excellent, Landon."

"Are you then saying that a godly life is founded in the Gospel through faith and union with Christ? So if we desire to do good works, we should pray that God increases our faith?"

"That's it my friend. No works? Then no faith. No faith, then no works. Essentially, the lack of good works come from a lack of faith. It is founded in unbelief. Consequently, if we want to do good works then we have to have true belief in Christ and if our belief is real then James 2 says we will have good works. Real faith produces works for the Lord.

Increase works? Then increase faith. Increase faith, then increase works. Using the understanding of the work of God, Jesus gave us a great picture of how faith is the chief grace given to us from God. Jesus said in John 6,

They replied, "We want to perform God's works, too. What should we do?" Jesus told them, "This is the only work God wants from you: Believe in the one he has sent." (John 6:28-29)

"So you see, Jesus here speaks as if there were nothing else required of us, but believing. However, in all of His wisdom, Jesus knows that truly believing in Christ springs all the fruits of the glorious Spirit. But the desire to want to do good works must come from the transforming power of the Gospel. Therefore, united with Christ, we will want to do good works because we love our Lord."

Everyone who was left in the Diner was now gathered around the table listening to the conversation.

"I guess the real trick now is increasing faith and our love for God," Landon said.

"Jesus told us how we are to do that."

"He did?" How?

"It is called the parable of the two debtors." Ethan opened his Bible and turned to the book of Luke. The Word of God declares,

Then Jesus told him this story: "A man loaned money to two people—500 pieces of silver to one and 50 pieces to the other. But neither of them could repay him, so he kindly forgave them both, canceling their debts. Who do you suppose loved him more after that?" Simon answered, "I suppose the one for whom he canceled the larger debt." "That's right," Jesus said. Then he turned to the woman and said to Simon, "Look at this woman kneeling here. When I entered your home, you didn't offer me water to wash the dust from my feet, but she has washed them with her tears and wiped them with her hair. You didn't greet me with a kiss, but from the time I first came in, she has not stopped kissing my feet. You neglected the courtesy of olive oil to anoint my head, but she has anointed my feet with rare perfume. "I tell you, her sins—and they are many—have been forgiven, so she has shown me much love. But a person who is forgiven little shows only little love." (Luke 7:41-47)

"The question is now, Landon. What do we need to hear to be shown our sin and know of the great forgiveness we find in Christ so we can truly love God with a great love because of our great sins?"

Landon smiled as he answered, "The Gospel."

"That is correct. We increase love for God with the power of the Gospel of Jesus."

"I'm satisfied," said Landon. "Everybody else think so?" Landon asked with a loud voice.

The people everywhere nodded their heads. Ethan stood up.

"Friends, I do know that down here in the underground we have to deal with problems in which we will never acclimate no matter how long we are here. However, ever since the creation of this world, mankind sinned eating of the tree, in doubt of the goodness of God and are infected by something we will never be able to acclimate to. We were not created to be in opposition to the living God who out of His love condescended to us all to share with us all of the wonders of His being. We were not created to be separated from our heavenly Father. The chasm was so large we could never on our best day reach the other side. We were doomed. The Creator of the universe could have left us in our unbelief, wickedness, and onto our judgment day. We have all sinned and fallen short of the glory of God.

"However, our good and loving God would not allow us to be condemned and separated from Him. He is a Father after all and what father will allow his child to be condemned and separated from him if he could do something about it. He sent his Son to come into this world to seek and save that which was lost. Jesus died for our sins, according to the Scriptures, and He was buried and He was raised on the third day, according to the Scriptures. Christ Jesus truly came into this world to save sinners. There is forgiveness for us today. Jesus fulfilled all that we failed to do, and He gives us all that He has received by His glorious work. There is salvation for you today. He has made a promise that all who call upon the name of the Lord shall be saved, and He promised that if you confess with your mouth and believe in your heart that Jesus is Lord, you will be saved. Jesus brings us life and life more abundantly and the Holy Spirit applies to us all that Christ has given. The Holy Spirit is here to give us power to overcome. We serve a wonderful God who loved us with an everlasting love. Right now He is calling us out of darkness and into His marvelous light. This is the promise of our heavenly Father, the God who does not lie, and all of His promises are yes and amen. Let us pray."

Ethan led the entire group in prayer. After the group amen, Ethan, Olivia and Landon with several others, talked with many who received the gift of faith that day, instructing them to celebrate the Lord's Day with them this upcoming Sunday at Salem Lutheran.

The group filed out of *the Diner* along with Ethan, Olivia and Landon.

"That was incredible," Landon said.

"Yeah. Never seen anything like that before," Olivia responded.

"That was truly amazing to see the Holy Spirit work that way," Ethan said, with a smile and watering eyes.

They walked to the front doors to get their scans and Landon stopped.

"Oops, I almost forgot. I got work to do."

Ethan and Olivia laughed. Ethan said, "I forgot all about it as well."

"Thanks you guys. It was a real blessing as always."

"You are very welcome, Landon," said Olivia

"And Landon," said Ethan. "Looking forward to eating breakfast on our island tomorrow."

"I'll make sure of it." Landon walked away in laughter.

8 THE LORD'S SUPPER

In the year of our Lord 2024, Singularity became a reality. The merging of man with machines brought unprecedented exponential change, catapulting the world into a brand new age of human progress. Basic lifestyles and the good life were radically transformed with brand new and unimaginable manners in which to live. Despite the new and apparent moral dilemmas that arose, most of the world's population embraced the developments and changed the entire landscape of the whole world. At the same time, many were still unconvinced and found that they could no longer function in the new world that Singularity built.

Jason Roland and his family sat at the table for lunch with each one of their heads bowed as Jason asked the blessing. Micha Jennings sat down at the table with them followed by Jeff Lee. *This is the Diner. It is the Law. You need it. Your neighbor needs it.*

"So everyone, we got hot dogs today," said Micha.

Grace, Jason's daughter popped up and said, "Hot

dogs are my favorite."

"Really?" Micha said. "I guess now that I think about it, they were my favorite food growing up, too. But it makes you kinda wonder though."

"Uh oh. Here we go," said Jeff.

"No. Hold on. This is a legitimate observation."

Jason and his wife sat with smiles on their faces awaiting Micha's presentation. They do truly enjoy the company of Micha and Jeff and love to watch their interactions when Micha shares his extraordinary thoughts.

Micha said, "Now we all have to assume that since there are no animals running around out here means that the meat we are eating is produced. My friend works in the Department of Health and says they actually clone the meat with the protein cells of certain animals."

"Yeah, we know this already," said Jeff. "Cow protein is used for our steak and hamburgers, and pig protein is used for our pork chops and bacon."

"Right. So check this out. I did a bit of research on hot dogs one day and found out that hot dogs were made of a grinding of all the left over meat trimmings. The trimmings are the parts you would throw away, if it were not for the hot dog. Some say that it is the lips, the ears, the eye-balls, and the tail. Stuff like that. Some will even say it may be a combination of the leftover parts of all kinds of different animals. Many will deny this." Micha lifted both of his hands in the air and shrugged his shoulders. "Either way, don't you think it strange that they make hot dogs here in Salem? Do we actually clone the trimmings and leftovers of meat to make hotdogs? That's like making recycled paper from scratch or making brand new pants with holes already in them."

"Wait," Jeff said. "How do you know they just don't clone the hotdog? Maybe they don't clone the trimmings and grind it, they just make the hotdog."

"I guess," Micha said. "But if they did that, then it would not taste like a real hotdog."

"Well have you ever tasted a real hotdog?" Jeff asked. "These hotdogs could taste like a cat for all we know."

"Gross!" Grace exclaimed.

"Anyway," Micha said. "Makes you kinda wonder about the other foods we eat."

"Just try not to think about it," said Jason. "Its not a good idea. You gotta eat the food. You really don't have a choice, unless you want to end up in Paradise."

"Yeah, I'm starting to feel sick to my stomach," Jeff said holding his stomach. "Oh." Jeff said as he held up his right hand and pointed upwards and then pointed to Jason. "Speaking of Paradise, a friend of mine from transportation stopped eating the food, and the council sentenced him to Paradise. They did not give him sixty days, though. It was kinda messed up, in my opinion. They took him right away."

"No kidding," Jason said.

"Yeah," said Micha. "We don't want that. We just need to think that we are getting what we need to live. We are getting all we need to survive."

"Ah." Jason puts his right hand up, getting everyone's attention. "But man does not live on bread alone. And, if we don't eat the body and drink the blood of Christ then we don't have life at all."

"Um… Jason, dude," Jeff said. "I thought we

were gonna stop making each other sick?"

"I was just responding to Micha's statement about only needing food to live. The Scriptures say we need the Word and the Lord's Supper to live."

"How so?" asked Jeff.

Jason reached for his Bible and turned to the book of Deuteronomy and read.

He said, "Deuteronomy 8:3 says,

Yes, he humbled you by letting you go hungry and then feeding you with manna, a food previously unknown to you and your ancestors. He did it to teach you that people do not live by bread alone; rather, we live by every word that comes from the mouth of the LORD. (Deuteronomy 8:3)

"This is also the Scripture Jesus quoted to Satan when He was tempted in the wilderness. We need more than food to live. We also, cannot just eat the miraculous manna from heaven as we wander in the wilderness to live. We must feed on the Word of God. We must feed on the Scriptures."

"Okay," said Micha. "Now, you are saying that as a figure of speech. Right? You don't mean we literally eat the Scriptures." Micha laughed.

Jason laughed and said, "Yes. Jesus meant that figuratively. Now check this out." Jason turned in his Bible to the book of John:

So Jesus said again, "I tell you the truth, unless you eat the flesh of the Son of Man and drink his blood, you cannot have eternal life within you. But anyone who eats my flesh and drinks my blood has eternal life, and I will raise that person at the last day. For my flesh is true food, and my blood is true drink. Anyone who eats my flesh and drinks my blood remains in me, and I in him. I live because of the living Father who sent me;

in the same way, anyone who feeds on me will live because of me." (John 6:53-57)

"Wait a minute, Jason. Now you are not saying that Jesus is teaching us about the Lord's Supper here directly. Are you?" asked Jeff.

"It was once said, by F.D. Maurice, of this passage, 'If you ask me, then, whether he is speaking of the Lord's Supper here, I should say, no. If you ask me where I can learn the meaning of the Lord's Supper, I should say nowhere so well as here.' I like this quote. It explains, beautifully, the meaning of the Lord's Supper and all that is wonderful concerning this very ordinance. But no, it is not specifically discussing the Lord's Supper here. At Salem Baptist Church, we have such a high view of the Lord's Supper, and so we partake of it weekly. The point of the passage of Scripture is why I say we need more than just the meals here at *the Diner*. We must also feed on the Word of God as well as the body and blood of Christ. It is what Christ has given His church as a means of grace. This is a means by which we grow and mature in Christ spiritually, like food does to the body physically."

"You know, it almost sounds like what I read concerning the Roman Catholic Church in the historical records," Jeff said. "They called it transubstantiation where the elements of communion actually became the body and blood of Christ. Is that what you are describing?"

"No." Jason took a drink of water. "We do not accept the teaching of transubstantiation, neither do we accept the teaching of consubstantiation. We disagree with Goldie and the members of Salem Lutheran concerning consubstantiation. We still love them though." Roland laughed. "In addition, we also, do not believe that the Lord's Supper is merely an empty symbol that we do in the sense of mere duty. Concerning the bread and wine, when Jesus said, 'This is my body' and 'This is the blood of the covenant.' It was symbolic of something, not nothing. It was symbolic yes, but it was not empty. What He is saying is that the bread is somehow His body, and the wine is somehow the blood of the covenant."

"For instance," Jason sat up in his seat, grabbed his empty plate and used it as a prop. "When Jesus says, 'I am the Door', he is not an actual door, but He somehow someway, acts as a real door. When Jesus says, 'I am the vine; you are the branches', He is not saying He is an actual vine, and we are actual branches. He is somehow someway a vine to us, and we are somehow someway branches. Jesus really is a door and Jesus really is the vine somehow someway. Now, when it comes to the bread, the presence of Christ is at the right hand of the Father, so it cannot be the literal presence of Christ here on earth. We do, however, affirm in our confession (1689 London Baptist Confession) that we spiritually receive and feed upon Christ crucified and all the benefits of His death. The body and blood of Christ is not physically, but spiritually present to our faith, as the bread and wine are to our outward senses. It is a real experience, spiritually, with Christ. Its awesome. We all want to have an experience with God and here we have it. The feeding of our spirits for us to grow, mature, and be empowered to the glory of the Lord Jesus. It is an awesome means by which He gives us grace."

THE DINER: WHY IS CHURCH IMPORTANT?

Jason began to speak louder and became more animated with his hand gestures. He continued, "That is why we take it every week. Essentially, what is happening here is a meal shared together with Christ and His people with all the benefits of being at the table of the Lord Jesus. What an incredible honor that is for us all. We, as the church, become united together around a wonderful meal set up by our Lord and are served by his ministers called to serve His people."

With a bit of a sarcastic tone, Jason said, "And people say we don't experience anything in church. Maybe that would be true if you don't take the Lord's Supper at all or you think it is an empty symbol."

"But as great as that sounds," said Micha. "Some will say we should not take it every week because it can become routine and meaningless. It may become a dull and a lifeless action. We don't want that."

"Now, I am not saying we have to take it every week to be right before God," Jason said. "We, however, should do it regularly. Once a month or once a quarter is not wrong as it is, technically, regular. Not sure though about once a year." Again, he voiced with a bit of sarcasm. "At any rate, we question no one who does not take it weekly. However, if it is taken less frequently because we are afraid that it will get dull and meaningless, then I would question. By that reasoning, we should not have the preaching of the Word every week because it could get dull and meaningless or I should not kiss my wife goodbye when I leave to go to work in the morning because it could become routine and lifeless. Hmmm." Roland put his right finger up and taped it against his right temple

"Ah. Point well taken," said Micha.

"I guess the real problem would be those churches who do not partake of the Lord's Table at all," Jeff said.

"Right," Jason said. "I would have an issue with that. Think of all that the people of that congregation are being withheld."

"In a way," said Micha. "It is almost like abuse."

Then Jeff Lee broke in the conversation with an inquiry. "I also read that some of the churches in the twenty-first century did not practice the Lord's Supper at all and did not preach or teach the Word of God in their services. If man does not live on bread alone, then it is like they were starving the people to death. I agree. Abuse for sure. I wonder why Christians allowed this to happen."

"Yeah, I would agree," Micha said. "If I knew of a child that was not given food to eat and was malnourished or was starving to death, I'm pretty sure I would have done something."

"Some might say it's not the same thing," Jason replied.

"Not the same thing?" Jeff asked, pausing briefly in thought. "On second thought, I would agree. It is not the same thing. It is actually worse. Withholding food kills the body, but withholding the Word of God and the Lord's Table kills the soul."

"Well many of the Christians were, in a sense, malnourished spiritually," said Jason. "That is why when the economic depression hit and the persecution came, many of them left the churches and the faith altogether."

"You're talking about 'The Great Apostasy of 2040?'" Jeff asked.

THE DINER: WHY IS CHURCH IMPORTANT?

"Right."

"Real quick," said Jeff. "Not to change the subject, but is it true that some of the twentieth and twenty-first century churches actually used grape juice instead of wine for the Lord's Supper?"

"Yes," Jason said. For all of church history, it was clear that wine was used for the Supper. When 'prohibition' came in the early twentieth century, the practice changed to grape juice and held steady for much of the twenty-first century. It all started because of the strong convictions of pietistic Protestants, and it continued to hold because of the overwhelming abuse of alcohol in those centuries by both Christians and non-Christians.

"Well, when we read the Bible, Jesus and the disciples actually drank wine during the Supper. Shouldn't we do the same, Jason?" Micha asked.

"Yes."

"Yeah, but I also read some teachings, that during that time, the wine did not have any alcohol in them. What of that?" asked Jeff.

"I heard that too, but it can't be the case," said Jason.

"Why not?" asked Jeff.

"Because Paul told the Ephesian church not to get drunk on wine. (Ephesians 5:18) Why would he tell them that, if you could not get drunk by drinking wine. How can you get drunk drinking something that does not have alcohol in it?"

"Ah. Touche."

"I guess I will have a different perspective when I take the Lord's Supper on Sunday," Micha said.

Jeff said, "Me too. I'm actually excited about it."

"Speaking of the Lord's Table, I have another

observation that I want to share with you guys," Micha said. "I think Christian's are where the idea for Vampires came from."

"Oh this ought-a be good," Cindy Roland said.

"Okay look, in the first century, Christians we very misunderstood by the Romans. The Romans thought that Christians were atheists because they did not have any idols in their homes and they thought they were incestuous orgy loving cannibals who were up to no good. First of all,"—he hits his right pointer finger into his left hand—"when Christians would gather they would celebrate the 'Love Feast' which was, essentially, the Lord's Supper and would greet each other with a 'Holy Kiss'. The Romans thought that Christians were having orgies in their meetings and because they called each other brother and sister, they thought it was incest. During the feast, the Romans would overhear the preacher quoting the words of Christ for the Lord's Supper. It lead them to believe that they were actually eating someone's body and actually drinking someone's blood. They thought they were cannibals. The Romans also thought they were up to no good because they met in secret meetings at night."

"This gave me a thought." Micha paused and scanned the table to make sure that everyone was still with him and had lost no one. Seeing that everyone was still with him, he continued. "Who do we know that will live forever and drink blood? Christians. If we stay out in the sun, Christians will get burned by the sun. If you drive a wooden stake into our hearts we will die. If you shoot Christians with silver bullets we will die. Put that all together, and we have the beginnings of vampires. The stories told about

Christians are the foundations for the legends of the creatures of the night."

"Yeah, but aren't vampires afraid of crosses?" Jeff asked.

"Yeah. I get stuck on that one. It's my only problem."

"And are they not supposed to be allergic to garlic?" asked Jeff.

"What's garlic?" Micha inquired.

"I don't know," Jeff said. "That's what they say in some of the old classic movies."

"It is a type of vegetable, I think," said Cindy.

"Oh. Well, if it is a vegetable then I am definitely allergic to it," Jeff said.

Micha said, "Look the problem is solved. Me too."

Jason's other daughter, Nancy said, "Me three."

"What are you guys talking about," Jason said. "You have to eat vegetables. You don't have a choice and I don't see any physical reactions with you guys from eating it."

"It's called the taste-bud rejection-itus!" Micha exclaimed. "It's a reaction in our mouths."

"Yeah," said Jeff. "Its when our taste buds negatively react to food that tastes bad."

Nancy said, "Yeah. I'm allergic to food that taste bad."

"Me too, daddy," said Grace.

"Thanks a lot you guys," Cindy said. "You're leading my children astray. Maybe you are vampires."

9 THE BENEDICTION

Life in Salem can be difficult for those who do not understand the various reasons for, what seems to them, an unnatural lifestyle. It becomes quickly apparent to many that we were not created to live underground, and the underground is all they have known. Much of the information known of the upside is that which have been handed down from generation to generation. Furthermore, there is no telling what else has been happening up there after all this time, and much of the stories told have fallen into the categories of myth and legend.

The younger generations have had to deal with many of the different hurts and struggles of the underground for reasons they cannot comprehend. As a result, it is only natural that they would desire to change the current situation; violently, if necessary. Zach Kelly, son of Victoria Kelly, is one such person. He regularly gets together with others who feel the same way, to discuss the possibilities of liberation.

Zach Kelly and Daniel Taylor sat at a table for

THE BENEDICTION

dinner. After Taylor, with his famous blue t-shirt on, asked the blessing, Zach cut into his pork chops.

"So pork chops and mashed potatoes on the menu for tonight," said Daniel.

"Yup," Zach said. "And, we got a small side salad, so it must be harvest time at the hydro-farm."

In Salem, vegetables are grown with special supplements in underground farms, using hydroponics and artificial sunlight generators. The department comprises of botanists, structural engineers and all their assistants. Zach Taylor is currently studying botany and after graduation, is to be placed in the hydro-farms of Salem. He is not happy about this decision. Yet, it is not the discipline. He very much enjoys the study of botany. Zach simply does not like the idea that he can't decide his future for himself. *This is the Diner. It is the Law. You need it. Your neighbor needs it.*

"So," Daniel said. "Your mom contacted me and asked me to set up a meeting with you. She sounds very concerned. Have you any idea what this is all about?"

"Let me cut to the chase," Zach said. "There are some of us here in Salem that are not happy about our current situation, and we think that we should fight for our place on the upside." Zach's voice trembled, and his volume rose. "We do not belong down here and we have just as much right to be upside as do the *syners*. Mom says, that out of all the people in Salem, you are the one who knows the most about the people upside. She said something about you actually knowing a *syner* who is also in the ministry."

The actual concept of *syners* being in the ministry

has always boggled the minds of those underground. They believe the whole idea to be a contradiction in terms. However, the Christian leaders in the underground Network believe this to be a wonderful illustration of who we are as Christians. They love to quote the great reformer, Martin Luther, that we as Christians are "Simul Justus et Peccator." Latin for "simultaneously saint and sinner." They demonstrate that before our Holy God, we as Christians still sin, yet, the righteousness of Christ is put on our account declaring us also, righteous.

"She is talking about Pastor Isaiah Scott who is a pastor on the upside." Daniel smiled and the look of reminiscing appeared on his face. "We came into contact when a fallen person whom they refer to as an 'apostate,' tried to dig his way down here. The rest of the story is classified, but I do know a thing or two about the people upside."

Zach is moved to excitement. Here is someone who knows a thing or two about the *syners*. "Is there any reason why we could not mount a force of people from the underground Network and fight to take back some land. Because we don't belong down here,"—Zach hit the table with his fist—"The way I see it. If I die up there, it is no different than being alive down here. I'm underground. That's where we are supposed to go when we are dead. So in a sense, I'm dead already."

"Okay, Zach. I hear you, my friend." Daniel spoke with a tone hoping to calm the passions that arose in Zach. "I do agree that we don't belong down here, but being down here is the best way for all of us to survive. In addition, an uprising would be futile. Even if you could muster a thousand soldiers, you could not stop even one of them. You will lose your life and accomplish nothing but bring more fear down to the *Network*."

Zach's face looked stunned. "I heard that their abilities were only a myth or a story to scare us to keep us from wanting to go up there."

"No," said Daniel. "I'm afraid the stories are real. The *syners* are faster, smarter, and much stronger than we are. They have merged with machines, and much of their bodies are made out of virtually indestructible synthetic materials. They can even repair themselves if you somehow manage to injure them."

Zach's face now turns into a look of desperation. "Okay, but since they are merged with machines, could we not stop them with an 'electro-magnetic' pulse or a digital virus of some sort?" he asked.

"Sorry," Daniel said. "They don't run on electricity, so to speak. Somehow they are powered by 'electrolytes' they get from liquefying the ice harvested from Europa, one of the planet Jupiter's moons. Again, a virus would be futile. We cannot comprehend the technology that they now possess. We don't know the programming language they use; if they even use programming language anymore. Even if we used all our resources to create a virus and somehow get it to take, at best, it might make one of them sneeze."

Zach, had the look of defeat. "You make them sound indestructible. I can't believe they are indestructible. There must be a weakness."

"I agree with you, Zach. They are not indestructible. However, we cannot do any of the destroying. We are powerless against them, and the only thing that could protect us from them is God

THE DINER: WHY IS CHURCH IMPORTANT?

Himself."

"So there is nothing we can do to get ourselves out of here?" asked Zach.

"Let me put it this way, my friend. The only reason we are even alive and are living down here in Salem is because they allow it. They understand our situation and our desires not to take part in their way of life. We believe it to be unnatural and sinful, and they respect that. We both knew that we could never co-exist, and so decisions were made to separate permanently. It was decided that the underground would provide the best chance for us to survive since the upside could not predict the environmental changes that would take place above ground, on land and in the oceans. When we first came down here, it was those on the upside who helped us create these underground facilities. They also helped us create the transportation systems, the hydro-farms, the air-recycling system, and all available resources available to sustain ordinary human life. So you need to understand that they were the ones who helped make it possible for us to continue in the way of life we desired."

"So what you are saying is, it does not matter," Zach said. "Even if we could fight to get land back and if we somehow, actually, got land back, we still may not be able to survive up there, since we do not know what the environment will be like."

"Yes," Daniel replied. "We have been down here a while. Our bodies have changed. With all the supplements and immunizations that we received over the centuries and the unnatural acclimation to our new environment, there is no telling what would happen to us if we went upside. There are probably new diseases, pollutions, temperature changes, atmospheric changes, radiation and countless other things we are not prepared for. The shock, alone, might kill us. And if we are able to breathe, for how long? It is folly." Daniel had the look of real concern on his face. "Zach, you are not the first to desire this and you wont be the last."

"You mean others have tried before?" Zach asked.

"Why do you think I know so much about the *syners*? How do you think it was that I came to know Pastor Isaiah Scott? While the apostate was trying to get in, I was trying to get out. Pastor Scott saved my life."

"So he killed the apostate?" asked Zach.

"Yes, but I know where you are going with this." Daniel cracked a little smile, knowing what was probably running through Zach's mind. He thought that Zach was probably thinking that it is possible for the *syners* to be killed. So all hope was not lost. He said, "Zach, you need to know that the pastors on the upside are essentially the enforcement up there. There is no one on this planet that is better trained in combat. No one can beat them. These guys are like superhero's up there, and they hold all the keys. One day, time permitting, I will even tell you about Samson. He was the first of them and single handedly changed everything up there. I know it may seem strange to you that they are pastors. We are not supposed to be like that." Daniel laughed.

"I guess they are a credit to your profession." Zach laughed.

"Yeah who would have thought that pastors could really kick-butt."

Zach sat there with a little smile, but it is obvious that

THE DINER: WHY IS CHURCH IMPORTANT?

he was deflated. He looked like he just ran a mile, with no sweat.

"Zach, my friend, we just need to understand that we are down here and we are truly blessed to be living in the best of all possible worlds."

"How can you say we are blessed?" Zach asked. "This is not a blessed life."

"I say it because you really do receive a blessing from God every Sunday at the end of service." Daniel held up both of his thumbs. "You really are blessed my man."

"Are you talking about when you say,"—he tried to use his best Pastor Daniel Taylor preaching voice—"may the Lord bless you and keep you? All that stuff at the end of the service?"

"Right."

"I just thought it was just something traditional and religious you guys like to say to end the service." Zach laughed.

Daniel Taylor with a smile, took out his Bible and put it on the table next to his tray.

"At the end of the service," Daniel said. "I remind everyone about the truths and promises that they have just heard and that they should go into the world confident of His care and His enabling. We are being sent, assured of the blessing of God. As Christians, we are truly blessed. The blessings come with a reminder that all authority in heaven and on earth has been given to Christ and in that truth, He has sent us into the world to make disciples of nations. I don't think that He sent us out there to fail. We are sent with His blessings."

"My mom says that this is one of the best gifts that can be given to a Christian," said Zach.

"Amen!" Daniel exclaimed. "The blessings in the Scriptures was always a big deal. We saw it with Isaac to Jacob and Jacob to Ephraim and Manasseh. And as a minister, I am an instrument by which God, the Creator of the universe, shows that He has favor on you. The blessing we give to you is because of the love Christ has for you, Zach. So no matter where you are, above ground, underground, you are living in the best of all possible worlds because God has favor on you. It cannot get better than that."

Daniel chuckled as if a funny thought had just popped into his mind. He continued, "Do you remember in school where the teacher seems to show favoritism to a particular student, and you all despised the student calling him a 'teacher's pet?' No matter what the student does, he or she can do no wrong in the teachers eyes. When the blessing comes, that is essentially what is being portrayed. You are one of God's favorites because of what Christ has done for us."

"I remember reading about blessings in the Old Testament." Zach said.

Daniel Taylor turns in his Bible to the book of Numbers

He said, "Good, cause the blessing you quoted a minute ago is found in Numbers. It says,

Then the LORD said to Moses, "Tell Aaron and his sons to bless the people of Israel with this special blessing: 'May the LORD bless you and protect you. May the LORD smile on you and be gracious to you. May the LORD show you his favor and give you his peace.' Whenever Aaron and his sons bless the people of Israel in my name, I myself will bless them." (Numbers 6:22-27)

"Moreover, we will see another beautiful picture of the blessing of the Lord."

Daniel Taylor turned the pages of his Bible. "In the book of Galatians, Paul declares,

Through Christ Jesus, God has blessed the Gentiles with the same blessing he promised to Abraham, so that we who are believers might receive the promised Holy Spirit through faith. (Galatians 3:14)

"This is the tremendous blessing of favor that God desires for His people. If God is on your side, who could ever come against you? It is like a person who wants to beat on you, but when he comes, he sees a big bodyguard standing behind you. He will think twice. Now, imagine that the Creator of the universe is standing behind you."

Zach Kelly imagined the whole scenario in his mind, and as he continued to eat his dinner, there appeared a little gleam in his eye.

Daniel continued, "That is what it means to really be blessed. There can be no greater blessing in the whole universe. This is what God desires to give us. This, my friend, is what we proclaim at the end of the service on the Lord's Day. You will walk through life with the name of Christ resting upon you and you and everyone will know it. When the minister gives the benediction and blesses, you need to know that you are truly blessed by God. What more in this world can you ask for. That is why I say, using the famous concept from Leibniz, that this world is 'the best of all possible worlds.'"

"Didn't Leibniz use this to solve the famous 'problem of evil' debate?" Zach asked.

"Yes," said Daniel. "You know, that is essentially the problem you are having with our current lifestyle."

"My issue is a 'problem of evil' issue? If God is a good God, why is there evil in this world?" asked Zach.

"Well, for the sake of time, just trust me on this."

Just then, the horn signaling the end of dinner sounded. Daniel Taylor smiled at Zach. This time Zach smiled back.

"You know what? I mean it man," Zach said. "Thank you very much. This time was actually very helpful to me and will be to my friends. I think I have a better outlook on my life now. No matter where I am,"—he pounds the table with his fist again—"I am blessed because God favors me. Thanks' again."

"No worries. Zach, anytime you need to talk, I'm here."

Daniel Taylor and Zach Kelly both got up to dispose of their recyclables and walked to the exit. They met up with Daniel's family and Zach's mom who were waiting for them so they could all get their scans together. This time at *the Diner* is not just the law. It is not just because it is good for you. It is also because it is good for others.

"Well, my son," said Victoria Kelly. "I have not seen you smile like that in a very long time."

"I'm happy," Zach said.

"And why is that?" Victoria asked.

Zach smiled, looked at Daniel and said, "I'm one of God's pets."

Both, Zach and Daniel laughed. Victoria had a look of confusion on her face as she looked at the rest of the Taylor family.

Victoria said, "I guess you had to be there."

THE DINER: WHY IS CHURCH IMPORTANT?

"I guess," said Michelle Taylor.

PART 3 - YOUR NEIGHBOR NEEDS IT

10 MEETING TOGETHER

In the year of our Lord 2099, the youngest son of the CEO of Titan Corporation decided that the new developments arising from Singularity were clearly immoral. Thomas Young, a graduate of the California Technical Institute and avid disciple of Christ, rejected the path set by Titan Corporation and its continued progress of machine and human integration. Young's ideology was shared by thousands of others who wanted a different lifestyle. Moreover, it became more and more obvious that the current society and environment could not sustain life for those who did not progress in the new technological era. There would need to be a new world created, specifically engineered to meet the necessities of life for those who would not be altered with the new technology. Thomas Young convinced Nicholas Knox, a major shareholder in Titan who also shared the same convictions, to help him develop a new underground colony conducive to their preferred lifestyle.

The Titan Corporation agreed to give Young and Knox their full cooperation in developing a state of the art underground facility equipped with all that is both comfortable and necessary to sustain human life deep below the surface of the earth. They created the *Network*. This is the combined connected structure of five underground cities: Salem, Zion, Bethel, Judah, and Eden. Thousands have found refuge in these cities, and thousands can live their lives the way they believe the Lord intended. In addition, thousands will eat at *the Diner* every day.

Louis Lopez and his wife Julia sat together for breakfast, and he asked the Lord to bless their meal. Newly married Marshall and his bride Jessica arrived at the table to join them. *This is the Diner. It is the Law. You need it. Your neighbor needs it.*

"Welcome back you two love birds," said Julia.

"Where did you guys end up going for your honeymoon?" Louis asked.

"We ended up going to Eden," Marshall said. "The director ended up giving us a great deal on a room at the front of their reservoir. Did you know that the water was heated, and you could get in the water directly from your room?"

"Maybe we should go there for vacation next time," Julia said, looking at Louis.

"Yeah well," said Louis. "I still can't stomach how the people in Eden can still drink that water knowing that people are swimming and doing who knows what in there."

"Eww." Jessica looked as if she just she gagged. "I think I just threw up in my mouth."

THE DINER: WHY IS CHURCH IMPORTANT?

Louis and Marshall laughed.

"You know Jessica," said Louis. "You do know what happens to all the sewage in Salem and what happens when it goes to the recycling pl—"

"Yes!" Jessica interrupted, slapping the table. "I know. Yuck. Don't remind me."

"You know Dad," Marshall said. "You would think that since we were born here, we would be used to the idea knowing of nothing else. But no. I think recycling our waste is naturally unnatural." Marshall snickered and Jessica blew him a kiss and mouthed the words, "I love you."

Just then, Eddie and Monica Nelson walked up the table with looks of utter frustration.

"May we join you guys?" Eddie asked.

"Sure," Marshall said. "Have a seat, you two."

Eddie Nelson is a transport mechanic who recently married Monica, who is an English Literature professor at the University. After a year of marriage, they are on the brink of separation and have recently stopped attending church services.

"So what have you guys been up to?" Louis asked. "Have not seen you two in a while."

"Well, we have been busy with lots of stuff," Eddie answered. "Trying to make sense of life."

"What's that supposed to mean?" Monica asked. "Are you saying you are trying to make sense of me?"

"No." Eddie blushed and wiggled around in his seat. "That is not what I meant. It's just that life is difficult right now."

"Oh. Oh. Sure." Monica's tone was dripping with sarcasm. "Life was easier before you married me. That's what you really mean."

"Sorry everyone." Eddie looked at everyone at the

table with the horrified look of shame on his face. "Marriage is kinda tough right now."

"Hey," Louis said. "No worries. It happens to all of us at times. Marriage is not an easy thing."

"At times it just feels impossible." Monica's voice trembled, and her eyes filled with tears.

Eddie said, "The long and short of it is,"—he nervously kept his eyes on Louis as he saw Monica's face turn toward him out of the corner of his eye—"she feels like I lied to her. I'm not the man she thought I was. She also said I led her to believe something about me that is not true. I know I'm not perfect, but I'm doing the best that I can."

"I just want the man I dated and was engaged to," Monica said. "It was like once we got married he stopped trying to engage with me. Everything he said he was, was all just an act. Don't you think that this deception is grounds to nullify our contract of marriage? We should be able to get an annulment or a divorce, right?"

"Well," said Louis. "I completely understand why you would feel deceived. I'm not sure I am convinced that Eddie's intention was to deceive you. But even if it was, you did not agree to a contract. You made a covenant with each other before the Lord our God when you got married. That's different."

"But I don't understand. If it is the case that he lied, even in a covenant, I should not have to stay with him."

"Not exactly," Marshall said.

Louis Lopez reached for his Bible and turned to the book of Joshua.

"Do you both remember the story of the

THE DINER: WHY IS CHURCH IMPORTANT?

Gibeonites?" Louis asked.

"I'm not sure." Monica at once remembered that pastor Louis told them both over and over again to read and remember that story in Joshua chapter nine.

"Well," said Louis. "Let me refresh your memory."—he smiled at Monica, as if he knew what she was thinking—"Joshua and the Israelites were going through the promise land and taking possession of it. The Gibeonites heard about what happened to Jericho and Ai and resorted to deception to save themselves. They told the Israelites that they were travelers from a distant country, that they did not live in the land, and that they traveled here to make a covenant with Joshua and the Israelites. After a little questioning, Joshua and the Israelites eventually made a covenant with them. It was, essentially, a peace treaty. Three days later, the Israelites found out they lived in the land. 'They lied to us,' they charged. The Israelites, however, did not attack the Gibeonites because the leaders would not let them. The Scriptures declare,

But the leaders replied, "Since we have sworn an oath in the presence of the LORD, the God of Israel, we cannot touch them. This is what we must do. We must let them live, for divine anger would come upon us if we broke our oath. (Joshua 9:19-20)

"So you see, a lie is not a reason to break a covenant. When you got married, it was indeed a covenant before God that you made. Till death do you part."

"That's not fair," Monica said.

"Yeah," said Marshall. "In the story, the Israelites did not think it was fair either. At any rate, Joshua and the leaders did, however, curse the Gibeonites and made them their slaves."

"The Lord will deal with Eddie if he did lie," Louis added. "However, I am still not convinced that he lied."

"Well, it does not matter now," Monica said. "It seems I'm stuck anyway you look at it."

"No matter what I do, it is never good enough for her." Eddie's voice became a bit louder, and he firmly tapped his fingers on the table. "She tells me that I'm constantly letting her down. I constantly fail her."

Monica quickly jumped in and said, "All he does, is go to work, come home, make a mess, ask me to be intimate with him, and make me feel guilty if I say 'no'. Even when we come to *the Diner* to eat, he does not say anything. He doesn't talk to me. He sits there and eats without a word. He treats me like I'm invisible."

"I'm just thinking about work." Eddie had the look of shock on his face with both hands in the air, shoulders shrugged, and mouth wide open. "We are under lots of pressure right now. I get home from work, and I am completely exhausted. And another thing, it's really hard to want to talk when the first thing I get when I walk in the door is constant nagging about how I failed at doing something at home."

"It's just common sense. Everyone knows this," Monica said, with the tone of disgust.

"Obviously not," Eddie responded.

"Ok," Louis interrupted. "Monica, you may need to know that Eddie really might not know what it is you are expecting. You should not have unspoken expectations. Don't assume that he knows. If you

THE DINER: WHY IS CHURCH IMPORTANT?

assume that he does, then you will think that he does not care about your needs if he does not do them. He actually may not know, and that is why it is not getting done."

"That's what I'm saying," Eddie adds.

"Now Eddie," said Louis. "It is important for you to know that though some of this may not be your fault, the whole marriage is your responsibility. You, my friend, are the head of the household."

"But, but you don't understand." Eddie pleaded with Louis. "She does not let me be the head of the household. She never has."

"Let me say it again. You, my friend, are the head of the household."

"I'm telling you."—shaking his head back and forth—"She won't let me."

"One more time. You, my friend, are the head of the household."

"Ok," Eddie said in defeat. "I'm obviously missing something."

"What we as men need to understand is that when we got married, we have become the head of the household," Louis said. "God sees you as the head of the household right now. Therefore, the question is not whether you are or are not the head of the household, because you already are."

Eddie had the look of confusion on his face as Louis spoke. Also, Monica looked at Louis with a crinkled forehead and her lips pulled to one side.

Louis continued, "Look at it this way. It is not about if you are the head or not; it is about whether you are a good one or a bad one. If you claim that you are not the head of your household, then you are saying that, right now, you will be a bad one. We might even say, right now 'I don't want to fail as the head of house, so I will not do it right now.' If you do that, you are failing right now."

"Ok," said Eddie, "I think I understand now."

Marshall added, "Eddie, here's the heart of it all. Christ has called us as husbands to love our wives as Christ loves the church. Remember, He died for His church. Therefore, you need to love her enough to die for her."

Louis jumped in, "The Scriptures say,
For husbands, this means love your wives, just as Christ loved the church. He gave up his life for her to make her holy and clean, washed by the cleansing of God's word. (Ephesians 5:26-27)"

"I see," said Eddie. "It is so hard to do sometimes when she acts the way she does."

"I understand," Marshall said. "However, Christ died for the church even when we act the way we do."

"That's a good point."

"And Monica," said Marshall. "Christ has called you to submit to your husband, even if he does not follow the Word." (1 Peter 3:1)

Louis read,
For wives, this means submit to your husbands as to the Lord. (Ephesians 5:22)

"That's hard to do when he is so unloving," Monica said.

"I too understand," said Marshall. "Nevertheless, you are to do it as unto the Lord not unto your husbands behavior."

"Gotcha."

"To put it plainly," Louis said. "The reason you both are miserable is that you both see each other as failing you. You both have a list of what your spouse is supposed to be like in your head and you are checking off all the areas where your spouse is failing you. You spend your day concluding that your spouse is failing you, and that is why you feel cheated and unloved. You then think that they should know better, therefore, you conclude that they are purposely failing you. Which makes you feel cheated and unloved. What needs to happen is a radical change in perspective. You both need to have lists of what you can do to be a better spouse and run down the list in your mind as to how you are being a failure to your spouse. You set out everyday looking for ways to be a better husband to your wife and wife to your husband. That is the key."

"That seems like it would be really hard to do," Eddie said.

"Yes. But if you do it, then you wont feel cheated; instead, you will desire grace and mercy. You will see that *you* are the failure and you will desire forgiveness from your spouse. You will see the Gospel in all of its fullness. We will see that our unfaithfulness to the Lord did not bring to us condemnation, but forgiveness. He had grace and mercy upon a people who did not deserve it. Christ gave us grace when we didn't deserve it. Are you able to extend grace to each other when they don't deserve it?

"Remember Matthew 18 and the parable of the unmerciful servant," Marshall said. "The servant who owed a master a large sum of money and was sentenced to be sold along with his family. But the servant begged the king for mercy and the king had pity on him, forgave his debt and let him go. After that, the servant went out and found a fellow servant who owed him some money. He choked him and demanded that he pay up. The fellow servant begged for mercy, but the forgiven servant refused and threw the fellow servant in prison. Other servants of the master saw what happened and told the master. Naturally, the master was outraged and called for the 'wicked servant'. He said, 'I canceled your debt when you begged me for mercy. Why did you not have mercy on your fellow servant?' The master threw the unmerciful servant in prison."

Both Eddie and Monica sat there with tears in their eyes holding each others hands. Everyone else, also sat silently as the Holy Spirit ministered to the hearts of Eddie and Monica. Eddie looked at Monica with a smile.

"I'm so sorry," he said. "I did not realize how selfish I have been. Please forgive me."

"I do. I, too, am sorry. I have also been selfish. Will you forgive me?" Monica asked.

"Of course I will."

"Aww," said Julia. "You guys are too cute. I love it."

Jessica Lopez, with tears welled up in her eyes, sat up and reached out to touch Monica's hands.

Jessica said, "That was one of the most beautiful things I have ever seen. I will be praying for you both."

"Jessica," said Monica. "My dear, we heard about what's going on. I will be praying for you both, especially when the time comes."

"Thank you very much." Jessica smiled.

"I have to say," Monica said. "When I heard the whole story, I thought that had to be the most romantic thing I had ever heard. Nice job Marshall."

"Thank you for your prayers. We are gonna need um," said Marshall.

Eddie broke into the conversation and said, "Thank you all for being here for us today."

"Today," said Louis, "you have seen the wonderful example of how the body of Christ supports, encourages, exhorts, and loves each other. That's why the church is here. We are here to encourage one another and to hold each other up in suffering."

"Yeah," Monica said. "I guess we kind of missed the point when we stopped coming to church."

"We need to keep meeting together," Louis said. "Not just for you, but also, for others. Other people need to see you there as well. It shows others you see the Lord's Day as important as they do and you show them they are important as well."

"When we come together," Marshall adds. "We 'spur' each other on in the faith. Truly, we cannot forsake gathering together."

Louis added, "The Scriptures declare,
Let us think of ways to motivate one another to acts of love and good works. And let us not neglect our meeting together, as some people do, but encourage one another, especially now that the day of his return is drawing near. (Hebrews 10:24-25)

"When the author of the Hebrews writes that they must not stop meeting together, it is a very strong admonition. Don't turn you back on the church. You need it and so does your neighbor. Essentially, the picture given in this passage is not simply neglect, but actual abandonment. The word here 'neglect' illustrates the forsaking of meeting together in covenantal terms, and the image is how Israel had forsaken the Lord and abandoned His covenant. As a result, this passage seems to suggest that those who abandon the church will be in danger of repeating the sin of Israel and abandoning the Lord. You don't want to be in danger of forsaking the church and ultimately the Lord Himself."

"We also have to remember that the church is identified with the Lord Himself," Marshall said. "When Paul the Apostle was persecuting the church in Acts nine, Jesus asked him, 'Why are you persecuting me?' He did not come against Christ Himself, but only His church, His people. However, Christ is telling Paul that if he comes against the church he is coming against Him. Beautiful picture of our union with Christ."

"You know," said Louis. "That is why I wonder about those who say they don't go to church, but insist that they still follow Christ. Rejecting the church is rejecting Christ."

"I guess we never looked at it that way," Eddie said. "It changes everything. Church is not just about us, but it is also about others."

"It is a lot like the Diner," Louis adds. "One of the reasons why our directors want us all to be in here together is to be an encouragement to each other. This time will show that this is important for you and important to everyone else that you are there. This is a time for us to be together to encourage and support each other in our lives here underground. This is a hard life, and we need each other. This is in essence what we are saying about the church. The Christian life is a difficult life and we need each other."

Everyone at the table sat again in silence to process all that had been discussed. Finally, Monica broke the silence.

THE DINER: WHY IS CHURCH IMPORTANT?

"Wow. This has been an incredibly enlightening day today. All of this over eggs and Canadian bacon."

MEETING TOGETHER

11 THE FAMILY

In the early twenty first century there was a prediction, that by the time 2050 was reached, the population in the world would be over ten billion people. In reality, the exact opposite took place. By the year 2020, the world's population stopped growing and rapidly fell at a faster rate than anyone thought possible. In the twenty first century, the rapid growth of the world's population caused a real concern that if the world continued to grow at this rate, the overpopulation would consequently, cause the depletion of every known life sustaining resource. It was, however, discovered that the problem was not that people were having too many children, but that people were not dying like they used to. The great progress of medicine was instrumental in clouding the world's judgments regarding its future. In actuality, many people in countries all over the world were having zero to one child per couple. Unfortunately, the world fell below the replacement rate of 2.1 children per couple. Humanity was not even replacing itself, much less multiply as God commanded.

To make matters worse, researchers presumptuously believed that if the world fell into this kind of decline, people would begin to have more children. They were wrong. No one wanted the lifestyle change that would come with children. "Kids are hard work and way to expensive," said many. Even when governments all over the world offered cash incentives and continued monthly financial support, there were no takers. Majority of the people, simply, did not want the "inconvenience" that would come with children.

Nevertheless, the breaking point began once the number of retirees outnumbered the number of workers, causing an economic stagnation and eventually, the economic collapse in 2099. If a couple only had one child, there would only be one worker to support two retirees. The math is simple. People lived longer after retirement, and as a result, a smaller working class was given a burden they could not bear. In addition, the divorce epidemic in the world would cause one child to essentially carry the burden of four parents. Social security, retirement plans, IRA's and Annuities did not, nor could not help. Society needed an actual economy for the retirement plans to have any value and provide the security intended. The economy collapsed.

Consequently, more and more women had to leave the home to contribute to the stability of the world economy. Eventually, the cost to survive became too difficult. When salaries would increase, the cost of day care and education would increase as well, making it more expensive for women to have a job than to stay home with the children. Rather than living with less, people just did not reproduce; looking to others to deal with the population issues.

Additionally, some even had the mentality that once they were dead, there would be no reason to care about the future of the world. The only reason to care about the future, is children. Why should they care about the future? For them, there is no future. No children, no care. Therefore, many in the world believed that someone who cares, would need to deal with the population crisis. Their minds would focus on the present, on themselves, no longer on the future, and no longer believing God when He calls children a great treasure.

Much to the surprise of many, it would be the latest breakthroughs of Singularity, toward the end of the twenty first century, that would end the utter demise of the human race.

LaMarcus Peters is the pastor of Bethel Baptist Church and a member of the board directors of the city of Bethel. Peters and his family sat at a table for dinner in *the Diner*, located in the center of the city. *The Diner* setup in Bethel is identical to that of Salem and like Salem, Bethel has the same requirements. It is the law. Before Seminary, Peters did his undergraduate work in Political Philosophy at the University of Salem and has been an integral part in governing the city of Bethel. After Seminary, he married his wife Camille and after five years, they have three children: James, Pricilla, and Naomi. LaMarcus Peters is handsome and tall with a muscular build. He is a male of African decent with unusually bright green eyes for his complexion and a goatee that is beginning to gray. He specializes in marriage and family counseling and is the head of the biblical counseling certification board for the entire network of cities underground. Peters is one of the most beloved in the city of Bethel. He asked the Lord to bless their dinner. *This is the Diner. It is the Law. You need it. Your neighbor needs it.*

After the amen, Bruce and Carrie Shultz, members of Bethel Baptist Church sat at the table to join LaMarcus and his family.

"Well," Bruce said. "Looks like we got chicken and rice tonight."

"It's my favorite," Carrie said, with a smile.

Bruce Shultz is the lieutenant of Bethel's security forces, and Carrie is an operator in the Department of Apparel, called in the underground, *the Mall.* Yesterday, they found out that Carrie is pregnant and requested a meeting with LaMarcus Peters to talk about the future.

"I guess congratulations is in order," LaMarcus said.

"Thank you," Bruce replied. "Again, thank you for meeting with us. We know that life will change a great deal."

"But," said Camille, "its going to be for the better. Remember, Psalm 127:3-5 says,

Children are a gift from the LORD; they are a reward from him. Children born to a young man are like arrows in a warrior's hands. How joyful is the man whose quiver is full of them! He will not be put to shame when he confronts his accusers at the city gates. (Psalm 127:3-5)"

Carrie said, "I guess when we watch our friends, how busy they are and how tired they always look, we keep thinking that having children may not be such a

THE DINER: WHY IS CHURCH IMPORTANT?

good idea even though we know that if we can reproduce, we are supposed to."

"But," Bruce added, quickly. "When we do ask them if they could do it again would they, they all say 'yes.' They say they cannot imagine life without them. I guess there must really be something about children."

"Truly," said Camille. "Truly a joy."

"Coming to *the Diner* to eat with my family is one of the best things in my life. I love this time," LaMarcus said.

"So after the breast feeding time period, we come to *the Diner*, and they have food made for our baby?" Carrie asked.

"That's right, and you will eat meals with your children every day," Camille said. "Three times a day. Something wonderful to share as a family. Just make sure you register your baby the week before you stop breast feeding."

"Interesting," said LaMarcus. "This is the desire of *the Diner*. Bethel understands the importance of the family structure and how it is vital to the child's development. We see the roles of the father and mother as the number one priority in the life of the child, and we do all we can to ensure that the structure stays healthy. Everyone on the council feels the same way about this, even those who do not share in Christianity."

"Yeah. Isn't that one of our core values at church?" Bruce asked.

"Yes," said LaMarcus. "But believe it or not, it has not always been the case with the church of the past. For years, children were separated from their parents during the church service, and the responsibility for discipleship rested on the youth leaders and youth pastors instead of their fathers. This practice contributed to the general disconnect of parents from their children in discipleship, and children eventually put their confidence in the institutions of the world instead of their own fathers and mothers. They would go to the institutions of the world for the answers to life's questions instead of their parents. Furthermore, the parents of that time, were of the same belief. They believed that the children need to go to the professionals, and they believed that they were not capable to help in the areas in which they were not considered experts. The church hired children's and youth pastors who were considered experts in these fields of child development. They celebrated that discipleship process."

"Sounds pragmatic," Carrie said. "What is right, is what works."

"But," Bruce added, "what was it that worked? All I see that worked was that parents were relieved of their God given duties to disciple their kids."

"It seems convenient for them," Carrie said. "Like everything else, they can blame someone else for the mistakes. If the child is not progressing in Christianity, it is not the fault of the parents; it is the fault of the youth or children's pastor."

"Like you said," added Bruce. "Pragmatism."

"Generally," LaMarcus said. "Pragmatism was a huge concept in the church of the twenty first century, and for many, they did not even know it. Pastor's were very concerned with the methods and models that would bring the desired results. The ends would justify the means."

THE DINER: WHY IS CHURCH IMPORTANT?

"Faith and practice should be directed by the Scriptures, not pragmatism. Right?" asked Bruce.

"Yes," LaMarcus replied. "This is why when it comes to the ministry of children, all churches in the underground Network have the children in their services and father's are intentionally equipped to disciple their children. This is the pattern we find in the Scriptures."

"Pattern? What do you mean by pattern?" Carrie asked.

"There is no Scripture that directs us specifically for our children to be in the worship services. There really is no 'thou shalt have thine children in thine services' Scripture, but we can see a pattern of children being a part of the assembly of God's people."

"For instance?" asked Carrie.

LaMarcus Peters reaches for his Bible and turns to the book of Deuteronomy. "The Word of God says, *Call them all together—men, women, children, and the foreigners living in your towns—so they may hear this Book of Instruction and learn to fear the LORD your God and carefully obey all the terms of these instructions. Do this so that your children who have not known these instructions will hear them and will learn to fear the LORD your God. Do this as long as you live in the land you are crossing the Jordan occupy."* (Deuteronomy 31:12-13)

"When the Word of God was to be read for instruction and commands, the children were to be there, in the assembly."

"But," Bruce said in disagreement, "that does not mean that there were young children there. It could be a reference to their older children."

"Ah yes," LaMarcus replied with a smile. "But you see the Hebrew word, here translated children, is 'taph' and it can be understood more literally as children who take quick tripping steps."

"I guess that sounds like little children to me." Bruce laughs.

LaMarcus turned in his Bible to the book of Joel.

"Blow the ram's horn in Jerusalem! Announce a time of fasting; call the people together for a solemn meeting. Gather all the people— the elders, the children, and even the babies. Call the bridegroom from his quarters and the bride from her private room. (Joel 2:15-16)

"Here we have another assembly and as we can see the children, as well as babies or nursing infants, were to be a part of the meeting with everyone."

"I know that it does not matter," said Carrie. "But I am curious if there are any Scriptures like these in the New Testament."

"Yeah, we got lots," LaMarcus said. "First of all, in Colossians we see,

Children, always obey your parents, for this pleases the Lord. (Colossians 3:20)

"The reason this is important, is that these letters by Paul were to be read to the church assembly. The Greek word for children is in the 'vocative case' which means, that it was a direct address. Paul is directly addressing the children in the letter read to the church, which means he expected the children to be at the meeting of believers to hear these words. Children were expected to be in the worship meetings, and we all need to be here for all of the blessings of grace that are given to us in the worship service. Don't you want your children to have the same blessing? Our Sunday morning services are for the worship of Christ and the edification of believers with the Lord's Table and the preaching of the Word of God. It is not simply an adult Bible study. Where the word of God is, Christ is there. Therefore, let us not keep our children away from Him. The Bible says,

> *But Jesus said, "Let the children come to me. Don't stop them! For the Kingdom of Heaven belongs to those who are like these children." (Matthew 19:14)*

Carrie continued to ask questions of LaMarcus, and while she did, Bruce flipped through the Scriptures looking intently for a passage.

"Okay," Bruce said, with a smile. "I just found it. I remember reading this and thought about it some. It says,

> *So on October 8 Ezra the priest brought the Book of the Law before the assembly, which included the men and women and all the children old enough to understand. (Nehemiah 8:2)*

"Does it not seem that the children who were there are to be those who could understand?"

"Great question," LaMarcus said. "Couple of things here. First of all, the passage is telling us who was actually there. We would have to assume a lot if we are to conclude that there were no children there who could not understand. A woman who could understand could have a baby in her hands and a man who could understand could be holding the hand of a child. Moreover, the passage does not directly tell us that the assembly excluded little children. Secondly, lets say that it does exclude them. Where were they? At home with babysitters? Is there a reason why the babysitters, who we would assume have understanding, were not at the meeting? What were they doing with the little children? Did they have a children's wing or a nursery somewhere? No matter what we may conclude, this passage in no way gives any pattern or principle for any program in the church that segregates children from the general assembly. This does not justify nurseries or children's church at all."

"I'm satisfied with that. Are you?" Bruce asked, looking at Carrie.

"Yes," Carrie answered. "You gotta think, though, I wonder if what we believe concerning the purpose of the church service affects what we desire to do with our children. I mean if we think that it is just a simple lecture on religion, then the time may not seem vital to our children. But if we see the service as necessary for the spiritual vitality of all of God's people, no matter what the age, then there would be no question."

Bruce said, in full support of his wife's statement, "If we believe that the Word being read and preached are the very words that spoke the universe into existence, then why would we not want our children there? If we believe that we are experiencing the forgiveness and assurance from our Lord in the service, then why would we not want our children to be there? If we are receiving the blessing of God given by the pastor in the benediction, then why would we not want our children to be there. Seems like a no-brainer." Bruce quickly put his hands over his mouth with the look of embarrassment. "Sorry, did not mean to preach." Bruce laughed.

Camille chuckled and gave her husband an affirming smile. She added, "We know that church is vital to the lives of Christians. Clearly, man does not

THE DINER: WHY IS CHURCH IMPORTANT?

live on bread alone. When I think about it, we would not keep our children away from *the Diner* to eat. Right? I mean I know down here it would be against the law. However, if it weren't, I'm sure we still would not keep them away. It's what's best for them."

"In addition," LaMarcus added. "We would not drop our children off to a place for them to draw pictures, color pictures, and play games, while we go into *the Diner* to eat for our physical survival. They need to be nourished for their survival, as well."

"And what about discipleship? You said that it is the parents?" Carrie asked.

"Does it not make perfect sense that it would be the parents?" asked LaMarcus, socratically. "The parents, essentially, teaches the child the basics of everything else. Why not God?"

"Nice point," said Bruce. "I suppose I would want my child to come to me with their questions concerning Christ. It would crush me to think my child thought I did not know enough about God to ask me questions."

"That is why we pour into the men at church," LaMarcus said, with passion. "We want to equip you to disciple your children and experience all of the blessings it will bring to you. The Bible says,

And you must commit yourselves wholeheartedly to these commands that I am giving you today. Repeat them again and again to your children. Talk about them when you are at home and when you are on the road, when you are going to bed and when you are getting up. (Deuteronomy 6:6-7)

"It seems that the Scriptures make it clear that it is the job of the parents to disciple their children. We, at the church, are here to assist you, not do it for you."

"You know, that all makes sense," said Bruce. "Children need the church like we do, and Carrie and I need to be diligent in preparing ourselves to disciple our child. I guess we both kinda got freaked out when we found out she was pregnant."

"It's true," Camille said. "Most people do freak out. And the first night you both go home with your baby from the clinic will be the most stressful experience of your lives. I remember, I could not sleep soundly. Every time James made a little noise while he was sleeping, I woke up and went to his crib to see if he was alright."

"I remember," LaMarcus said, "I was always worried, when they were so still while sleeping, that I watched their chest to make sure they were still breathing. I also remember, we had to contact a medic three hours after we got home because we panicked. Do you remember why?" LaMarcus looked at Camille.

"I can't remember why. But you know what,—she looked at both Bruce and Carrie—"just read your pamphlet while you are at the clinic, and you will feel much better."

"Already ahead of the pack," Bruce said. "I read all the recent studies warnings in the pamphlet. Making sure to lay the baby on its back to sleep and the correct ways to handle the baby. You have to wonder though, with all this new found studies that are life and death important, it kinda makes me wonder how in the world any baby before this century ever survived." Bruce laughed.

"No kidding." LaMarcus had a large smile on his

THE DINER: WHY IS CHURCH IMPORTANT?

face, looking like he could remember thinking the same thing.

Just then, Carrie with the look of real concern on her face asked, "I didn't want to bring this up, but is the 'Choice' issue something to be concerned about?"

The whole demeanor of the table changed. The "Choice," as those in the underground have come to call it, has been a difficult choice indeed. Abortion is illegal in the underground; however, if there are projected harmful complications with the pregnancy or if there are potential birth defects, then there is an option for termination. Because food and water have become the most precious and limited of resources, it cannot be given to those who are "unfit" to contribute to the Network. If a child is born with a considerable defect, it will immediately be taken to *Paradise*, where the parents and the child will spend their last moments together, as the baby is withheld nourishment and given sedatives. Essentially, the infant starves to death. The trauma for the parents has had serious effects on their mental stability. It has even led to suicide. The governing body legalized the termination of the pregnancy in these instances to spare the parents of the overwhelming grief. Thus, the "Choice." Terminate the pregnancy or watch your baby starve to death.

"Okay," said LaMarcus, "if it does come to this, we believe that the parents should not terminate the pregnancy, as we believe, as I know you do, in the sanctity of life and that our God is able to work a miracle. We want to give the child every chance to live and every chance for God to bring Himself glory. However, in the event that a miracle does not happen, we must understand that our life here on earth is that of a 'pilgrim,' and our home is a heavenly one, built by our Lord. This time, is a time of suffering and hardship, but we can overcome the world because Christ did. We can do all things though Christ who will give us the strength. We will pray for you and support you as your church family during that time believing with all of our hearts that Christ will carry you through the fire."

Bruce and Carrie both sat in silence with the look of deep thought and fear.

Finally Camille said, "Hey you two. This is a time of excitement. Just make sure you guys follow the instructions and take your pregnancy supplements, Carrie. Take care of yourself and you will take care of the baby. All things were made through Him and for Him,"—she pointed up—"so He will hold everything together. Have faith in our Lord Jesus, all things will work for together for our good. Okay?"

"Okay," said Bruce.

"Thank you both very much for helping us," Carrie said.

"You will be in our prayers," Camille responded.

"Love you guys," LaMarcus said with a smile.

With that, the families disposed of their recyclables and made their way to the front to get scanned. As Bruce and Carrie Shultz waited for their turn to be scanned, they looked at all the children and babies sitting, eating, and laughing with their parents. Smiles appeared on their faces as the excitement stirred within them. Bruce then looked at the bottom of an infant being held by her mom and wondered about waste disposal in Bethel. When he was young, he remembered asking his dad about where all the waste goes in the city. He also remembered what his dad said, "you don't want to know." He shuddered.

12 BE THE CHURCH

In the year of our Lord 2040, hundreds of thousands left churches all over the world. Congregations did not just dwindle overnight, they completely disintegrated, and in the aftermath, it was understood that there were two primary reasons for the "Great Apostasy of 2040." The first reason was a severe economic depression in the leading economic countries of the world. The second, was the official "illegalization" of "intolerant" Christianity in many countries all over the world.

For the most part, Christian churches, especially those in the western world, did not strive to bring about maturity in their attenders with as much effort as they did in getting them to consistently attend. In the late twentieth and early twenty-first centuries, many congregations became so concerned with the quantity of their attenders, that they neglected the quality of their members. Consequently, any professing Christian at the time, did not have the maturity nor the perseverance to withstand the hardships beginning to appear.

Sadly, the Scriptures were not being taught, the Lord's Supper was not being served, and church discipline and biblical discipleship were neglected. To a greater extent, the pastors of these churches were more concerned with "entertaining goats" than "feeding the sheep," figuratively speaking. Making matters worse, the people of those churches wanted it that way. The Scriptures in Jeremiah became the common declaration.

A horrible and shocking thing has happened in this land—the prophets give false prophecies, and the priests rule with an iron hand. Worse yet, my people like it that way! But what will you do when the end comes? (Jeremiah 5:30-31)

The pastors of those churches said what they wanted, did what they wanted, and the people loved them for it. And just like the end came for the Kingdom of Judah, the end came for them.

In light of it all, what became apparent was the premise that the sheep of Christ would hear His voice only and they will follow none other. What is it that we should conclude of those who would attend churches where the voice of Christ was not declared? Sheep or Goats? Eventually, many of these professing Christians—the goats—concluded that the promises of prosperity and the good life were all a lie and that all these years were a tremendous waste in light of the economic depression. They were hearing a message that Jesus would save their lifestyle, not their very lives, and therefore, when they lost their lifestyle, they lost their faith and their very lives.

In addition, the wave of tolerance that swept over the world continued to shape policies and interpretations of constitutions. In the spirit of tolerance, society continued to grow progressively intolerant of those who were intolerant. Absurdly, it became a hate crime for Christians to lovingly say that Jesus was the only way to the father, to say we are all sinners, to insist that there is a hell, to declare that God is wrathful, to define marriage as a union between a man and a woman, to say that the Bible is the only Word of God, and to say that Jesus rose from the grave. Because of the intolerance of those who claimed to be tolerant, the consequences were dire. Heavy fines, repossession of property, loss of retirement, prison and even death in some countries. Few professing Christians in the west would undergo that kind of punishment for their faith, and they would, inevitably, attend churches that would compromise their doctrine in light of the progress of society. However, compromise does not inspire and as a result, people eventually just stopped going to church altogether. All of this would contribute to the mass exodus.

Thankfully, Christianity would not stay down for long. The long term results of Singularity would have catastrophic effects on human development. When human potential was increased, everything man was capable of doing was brought to a whole new magnified level. The increase was not just intelligence and strength, but also, sin. Sin now had the power of a machine behind it. Again, the results were unexaggeratedly cataclysmic.

It was only the truths of Scripture, the preaching of the Gospel, the Lord's Supper, Baptism, confession and assurance, the invitation, the benediction, the love and support of ministers and other fellow Christians, and especially, the power of the Holy Spirit that would quench the exponential progression of sin in the era of Singularity. Christianity would rule the day as long as it was authentic Christianity. The church had to be the church period, and nothing less would be accepted.

Ethan Gold and his wife were having dinner together when they were joined by Tristan Cooper, the lead guitar player for the band *Hunger*. This is a rock band, from Judah, that travels to all five of the cities' underground to entertain, and though Cooper is resident of Judah, he is playing a show in Salem. No matter where you are in the Network, *the Diner* is the law.

Tristan was very excited to go to *the Diner* in Salem this day, because he would join his friends Ethan and Olivia for dinner. *This is the Diner. It is the Law. You need it. Your neighbor needs it.*

"So Tristan, does the chicken here in Salem taste like the chicken in Judah?" Ethan asked.

"I think so. You all use a different marinade though. Well, at least I think it is a marinade." Tristan thought for a quick moment. "Now that I think about it, it might be the chicken. But isn't all the chicken made from the same cells?"

"That is my understanding," said Ethan.

"It has to be the food," Tristan said. "When we are traveling, I get the runs when I eat in Salem. It's either the food or the water."

"Could be the air," Olivia responded. "We get really bad sulfur levels sometimes."

"No way!" Tristan exclaimed. "Zion, by far, has the worse sulfur levels. When we were there, everyone in the band got sick during breakfast."

THE DINER: WHY IS CHURCH IMPORTANT?

"What were you guys eating?" Ethan asked.

"Eggs." Tristan laughed.

"Well, that makes sense." said Olivia, with sarcasm. "They just need to quit serving eggs down there."

Tristan nodded and smiled, as if his Attention Deficit Disorder had moved his focus on to something or someone else.

"So where are you guys playing tonight?" Olivia asked, trying to get his attention.

"Uh,"—he refocuses—"We are playing a new venue here called, 'the ladder.' I guess it just opened a month or two ago. It's supposed to be pretty nice."

"Yeah," Olivia said, "We went to check it out last week. We saw 'H2O' that night.

"How were they?" asked Tristan, with a little tone of insecurity.

"They were pretty entertaining. Nice place."

"Oh, did they serve drinks that night?" Tristan asked, with eager anticipation.

"No. They can't do that. It's against the law," Ethan answered.

"Yeah, but we heard when we were playing in Zion that the evening venues in Salem might be allowed to start serving drinks."

"Well we heard nothing like that," Olivia said.

"Do you guys think that the manufacturing departments will figure out how to make alcohol, other than wine, again?" Tristan asked. "I was reading, in the historical records, that the evening venues in the twentieth and twenty-first centuries served all kinds of alcoholic beverages, and it made people a bit more relaxed. I guess alcohol can be made with other foods beside grapes. I also read that it helped the bands get things going."

Ethan responded, "The problem will be regulations. As a Pastor, I love being able to serve real wine when we serve the Lord's Supper. The problem with the service of alcoholic beverages in, lets say, recreation settings, is that it tends to be abused. People tend to get drunk. As least that is what I read in the historical records. Drinking alcoholic beverages may not be a sin, but drunkenness is."

"Well either way, I hope they at least let the venues serve water. It will give the people something to do other than sit and stare." Tristan laughed. "Also, I can almost imagine people sitting with white burning sticks in their mouths and occasionally blowing out smoke. I don't know why I get that picture in my head sometimes. Anything, to get people to like our music." Tristan laughed again.

"I thought everyone loved your music," Ethan said.

"Not everyone," Tristan replied. "We tend to be a bit edgier than other bands. Most of our shows are full of younger people. No offense you guys."

"None taken," Olivia answered. "We like your music so that must mean we are"—she made the quote motion with her hands—"younger people."

"Or it means that we suck."

Olivia laughed. "Why do you say that?"

"Well, you guys are part of the older generation. No offense again. Like my parents age. We have a saying. The day our parents think our music is cool, is the day we truly become uncool."

"Ok. So do your parents think you are cool?" Ethan asked.

THE DINER: WHY IS CHURCH IMPORTANT?

"Yes."

Everyone at the table laughed, getting some at other tables to take notice. They even started to wave at Tristan Cooper. Tristan waved back.

"I think the real reason—he brushes his hair out of his face with his finger—"that they think we are good is because mom and dad are reading these psychology articles urging them to be supportive and encouraging to their children."

"So in this case, it would be less encouraging to be encouraging." Olivia laughed. "Well, that's what you get from reading psychotherapy articles."

"You ain't lying," Tristan said.

"You know I've been thinking about what you just said, Tristan," Ethan chimed into the conversation after he seemed to be in thoughtful deliberation.

"What? Which part?"

"Your saying."

"Oh," Tristan said. "The day our parents think our music is cool, is the day we truly become uncool."

"I was thinking that I could use it too. It would be a good illustration for the church."

"Really?"

"Yeah. I'll give you credit of course."

"Nah, that's okay," Tristan replied. "I think we stole it from another band."

Ethan stated, "The day the world thinks we are cool, is the day we become uncool. And what I mean is the church actually becoming uncool in God's eyes."

"You gonna elaborate more?" Tristan asked.

Ethan Gold sat back in his chair lightly tapping his lips with his fingers. While he sat thinking, everyone else at the table sat in silent apprehension as they continued to eat their dinner.

"What I believe I'm wanting to communicate is at the very core of what we could call, if you will, our 'identity,'" Ethan said. "We would say that the chief end of the church is worship. Just like we always say, 'the chief end of man is to glorify God and enjoy Him forever'. Now if the chief end of the church is worship then, we should make sure that worship is really happening. At any rate, if we look at church history and look some of the temptations we face today, we would see that many may think our chief end is evangelism."

"Huh? Wait a minute Ethan. What's wrong with that. Isn't evangelism good?" Tristan asked.

"Yes. But evangelism, in the wrong context can be unproductive."

"To me it seems wrong to think that there could be a wrong context for evangelism."

"I know that this may sound a little weird," Ethan said. "But the church service would be the wrong context."

Tristan Cooper's jaw dropped and even Olivia's eyebrows, lifted a little.

"Okay. Bear with me a little. Now I am not proposing that evangelism can't or should not happen during Sunday morning services. It's just not the primary purpose. Generally speaking, we come together to worship the Lord, to receive the blessings from the Lord, to be Baptized, to be fed the Lord's Supper and to be fed the Word of the Lord on Sunday mornings. We are to gather, as believers, the people of God, to worship the Lord in spirit and in truth.

"In the past, churches lost sight of this and turned

the worship services into outreach events appealing specifically to those who are not Christians. In order to do this, the church started to become more and more like the world and less and less like the church. The same day the world thought the church was cool, was the day the church became uncool in God's eyes."

"I got it. Let me ask though. Is it always the case that the world thinking we are cool is a bad thing?" Tristan asked.

"Only if we are changing who we are to make them like us. Just like how it would be if you changed your music so that your parents will like it."

"We can't do that. We would lose our fan base. They would definitely think that we were uncool. If people are going to like us, they have to like us the way we are because we need to be who we are, to be who we are. Wait, did that make any sense?"

"I think so." Olivia laughed

"Yes," Ethan said. "It's kind of the same thing. If we stop being the church then who will be the church? There needs to be a church. We have a world already. We don't need the church to be the world, we need the church to be the church. It is the church that God instituted to disciple the people of God. To baptize them. To teach them to obey everything that the Lord commands. Where else will they go? If you guys stop playing your kind of music, what will the people who like your music listen to?"

"Nice juxtaposition Ethan," Tristan said with a smile on his face. "I was waiting for an opportunity to say that word."

"I don't even know what it means." Olivia said.

"Basically, it means putting two things side by side

for the purpose of comparing or contrasting," Landon replied.

"Great word," said Ethan.

Landon nodded his head with a grin. "Okay focus. But will not some say that discipleship is supposed to happen in the small groups, not necessarily in the worship services. All the Bible studying and the necessary fellowship should happen in the small groups. Right?"

"Small groups provide a necessary service to the discipleship process of Christians," Ethan answered. "However, it cannot take the place of a Christ-Centered worship service."

"You know what is interesting to me," Olivia said. "When this kind of practice is going on, I wonder about the leaders of the groups. Many of the small group leaders are tasked with encouraging and discipling the people of God. However, it was the pastor, not the small group leader, who went to Seminary and was trained for years in Christian discipleship and formation. The small group leaders were not trained for this task, and they are held responsible for any of shortcomings in spiritual formation? Unthinkably, the pastor is not doing the discipling, but doing the very thing everyone else can and should be doing."

"I am assuming," Tristan said, "you believe that we bring people to church so they can hear the pastor preach an evangelistic presentation, but we can do that same presentation on our own. We can evangelize everyone, anywhere. But where do Christians go once they are saved to be discipled if not the church, served by an ordained pastor called and trained in the ministry? We can lead people to

Christ and our pastor leads us into maturity in the worship services. Is that what you mean?"

"Yes sir," Olivia answered.

"Exactly," Ethan said. "Consequently, what will happen is that we will urge the church and pastor to tone down everything, so that we don't offend the people we bring. The church does not declare the truth, the whole truth, and nothing but the truth, because the message of sin and the cross of Christ is offensive to unbelievers. This causes the unbelievers that came to the service to hear an adjusted Gospel, which is no Gospel at all, and at the same time, the Christians that came are not equipped. The Scriptures declare,

Now these are the gifts Christ gave to the church: the apostles, the prophets, the evangelists, and the pastors and teachers. Their responsibility is to equip God's people to do his work and build up the church, the body of Christ. (Ephesians 4:11-12)

"It is not the work of the congregation, but the work of the pastor to equip. How will we able to do His work if we don't even know what that is? How are we to build up the body of Christ without the power of the Gospel proclaimed and the Scriptures taught? We do a disservice to the people and most importantly God, when we do not do what He has commanded us to do. We need to be what He wants us to be, and He wants us to be the church. The church can be so preoccupied with appealing to the unchurched that we neglect the responsibilities God has given us."

"I think some may say," Tristan said, "'that's the problem.' When the church is what it is supposed to be, it is kinda boring. It's not really entertaining.

That is why things are changed, because no one will want to go to a church being what it is supposed to be. I mean if the Christians don't even want to be there, why would unbelievers come? People think that the church is uncool and we need to be cool if people will attend."

"Yup," Ethan replied. "I understand. But the church is more about what we need, then what we want. We don't exist for attendance, we exist for worship. It is not our goal to be cool to the world, but to be obedient to God. For instance, it would be nice if we came to *the Diner* every day and ate cookies, chocolate bars and everything that taste good, but have no nutritional value. If we did this, everyone would be happy eating what they wanted, but would eventually become sick and die in no time. We have to eat what we need, not what we want. With regard to entertaining, that's what the entertainment venues in Salem are for."

Tristan Cooper laughed. "Nice."

"Seriously though," Ethan said, with real concern. "The purpose of *the Diner* is to feed us what we need to survive. Whether it has wonderful decor, good music, the perfect temperature, nice restrooms, or cool people, it would not matter. We are not there for that. It is the same with church. We are there to worship the Lord and to receive grace and knowledge from our Lord. What if the Diner had the best decor, best restrooms, best screens and the best everything, but had no food? Would go there to eat? What if the church had all the best amenities, but no true worship or the preaching of the Word of God. Would we still go there to worship? If you still go, you are saying a lot more about yourself than you think."

THE DINER: WHY IS CHURCH IMPORTANT?

"Wow," Tristan said, "it seems that our misunderstandings as to the nature of the church is causing us to rob ourselves of the blessings of the Gospel."

"Yes. That is why we need the Scriptures, to know the true nature of the church, so we can really be the authentic church. Anything else would be the creation of man, and if that is what we believe, then really, who cares. We might think that it is a good thing to do, but not something essential for our spiritual and physical vitality. It is all an option."

"So," said Tristan, "the church is very much like the Diner."

"Exactly," Ethan said. "If the Diner is not what it is supposed to be then we are all in trouble. We need it to be what it is supposed to be to survive. It is the same with the church. This is why I say, the day the world thinks we are cool is the day we become uncool."

"I think it is natural for the world to reject the true church and think we are uncool." Olivia said.

"Yes, the message of the cross is an offense," Ethan replied. "The existence of the church is a reminder of the looming judgment that is coming and the natural disposition of the world is to reject the true church. Therefore, if those who reject God, like you, then something might be wrong. The Scriptures declare,

"If the world hates you, know that it has hated me before it hated you. If you were of the world, the world would love you as its own; but because you are not of the world, but I chose you out of the world, therefore the world hates you. (John 15:18-19)

"The church is a reminder of the God they believe

in, but are rejecting."

"Wait. Are you saying that everyone in the world believes in God?" Tristan asked.

"Yes. Everyone believes in God. The problem is that they rebel against him. I like to say it this way, it is not that they don't believe in God, it is that they won't believe in God. Romans chapter one makes this point very clear."

"Go on," said Tristan.

"The problem is not the existence of God. When we look in the Scriptures, when it comes to unbelief, it is never addressing the existence of God, but the goodness of God. We, inherently, don't believe that God is a good God and has our best interest in mind. It is similar to the temptation in the Garden of Eden when the serpent led Eve to doubt the goodness of God and doubt that He had our best interest in mind. For yet, another example, the Israelites wandering the wilderness after they were delivered from Egypt. They knew that God existed, how could they deny that? However, when they were in the wilderness they complained in unbelief thinking that God only brought them out of Egypt so that He could watch them die in the wilderness. They doubted the goodness of God. The problem with unbelief in God, is that it is a moral issue. Unbelief is a sin that God holds us all accountable to. We think that people are not Christians because they don't have enough information, but it is because they reject the truth and exchanged the truth for a lie in rebellion. They absolutely believe in God, they just hate Him. They believe He is an awful God. Look at this passage."

Ethan turned in his Bible to the book of

Revelation. "The Scriptures declare,
There was a terrible hailstorm, and hailstones weighing as much as seventy-five pounds fell from the sky onto the people below. They cursed God because of the terrible plague of the hailstorm. (Revelation 16:21)

"Now what is important here is not your view of eschatology, but the fact that people at the very end of it all still had hatred for God. The final bowl of the wrath of God is being poured out and what are the unbelievers doing? They are cursing God. They are about to die and with their very last breath they curse God. Why do they use their last breath to curse a God that they don't believe exists? They despise their Creator so much, that they desire their last moment of life to be one in complete defiance. Again, It is not that they don't believe, it's that they won't believe. They utterly doubt the goodness of God."

"Aren't we guilty of that? Don't we do that today?" Tristan asked. "I think we do, even as Christians."

"All the time," Ethan answered. "When we have a need, sometimes we don't pray because we don't think it will work. Sadly, the reason is not that we don't believe God exists, but that we don't believe God will help. I like to say it this way, it is not that we don't believe that He can, it is that we don't believe He will. We also think that God is there standing behind us watching our every move, and waiting for us to do something wrong so that He can immediately punish us. We doubt His goodness in thinking that His motivation is to punish us rather than show us His wonderful grace. We doubt, His goodness. As Christian's, what makes us different is not that we believe that God exists, but that we believe He is good. That is the essence of true faith. Even demons believe God exists. Furthermore, this shows us so clearly that our biggest problem is not life underground, but unbelief. Oh you of little faith (Matthew 8:26)."

"Whoa." Tristan had the look of surprise. "If it is like that even for Christians then what about the unbelievers in the world."

"I guess that answers the question as to why the world does not like us," Olivia added.

The tables began to clean up their areas.

"Well, I guess I better get back to our room," Tristan said.

"Where is the rest of the band?" Olivia asked.

"They are at the table over there. Do you see them? They are waving to us right now."

"Oh, Yeah. I see them. Hi." Olivia smiled as she waved to the rest of the band.

"Thank you guys very much for the enlightening conversation," Tristan said, with true gratitude. "The true church is vital for sure. Thank you for being faithful."

"You are very welcome." Ethan smiled at Tristan.

As they all stood to take their trays to dispose of their recyclables, they were joined by the rest of the band. After all the hugging, they all moved toward the front of *the Diner* to get scanned.

"So what time is the show tonight?" Ethan asked.

"Nine tonight. I think." Tristan looked at the rest of the band for confirmation. He got it.

"I think we are going to bring some of the young children from the church tonight. Pass their bedtime for sure." Olivia laughed.

THE DINER: WHY IS CHURCH IMPORTANT?

"We will help keep them awake," Tristan said, in jest. "It should be somewhat loud."

"You guys still sound depressing?" Ethan asked.

"We are not depressing. We are melancholy," said Tristan, sarcastically.

"Oops. My mistake." Ethan laughed and put both hands up in the air acting like he was embarrassed. "Well, we're looking forward to it."

"All the other pastors in Salem coming?" Tristan asked.

"I don't know," Ethan answered. "I do know that Louis and Marshall will not be there tonight. Marshall's new wife Jessica went into *Paradise* last night. It's just a matter of time now."

"Aw," Tristan said, in grief. "I was hoping to meet her. I better go see Marshall later."

"Daniel Taylor said that he might come," Ethan added, trying to change the subject. But I think that means he's not coming.

"Daniel still cracks me up," Tristan said. "And what makes him even more funny, I know he's not even trying."

"I know what you mean." Ethan stepped up to get his retinal scan.

"Thank you, Reverend Gold," said the scan operator. "Great job preaching the Gospel in *the Diner* the other day."

Ethan smiled. "God is good."

"All the time."

The Gold's and the band *Hunger* all walked out of *the Diner* together like one big happy family. As they walked out Ethan asked, "So anyway, you guys want me to do some 'roadie' work for you tonight? I learned to tune a guitar last week."

"Still trying to join the band?" Tristan asked, looking at Ethan with a grin.

"Well, what if I do, will that make you uncool?"

CONCLUSION

Micha Jennings walked out of *the Diner* and headed toward the East Wing tunnel in the city of Salem. Before he entered the East Wing, he saw Marshall Lopez walking out of the Department of Health with tears in his eyes, and he thought to himself that Jessica must have died. Sympathetically, he walked up to Marshall, gave him a hug and said nothing. It was truly a loving moment of silence.

After the embrace, Micha proceeded down the tunnel in the East Wing, with sorrow in his heart for Marshall. He looked intently at the steel walls to see if the structure would somehow reveal the location of the accidental tunnel that was dug leading out to the upside. While Micha inspected the walls carefully, Zach Kelly walked toward him from the East Wing like a curious child. He wondered what Micha was doing as he scanned the walls recording data in a notebook.

"Hey, so, what-cha doing?"

"I'm just checking out the structure of the tunnel."

"So you with engineering?" Zach asked.

"Um. Yeah." Micha responded, with nervousness.

"Aren't you guys supposed to be in uniform and wearing your badge on your sleeve? I think you guys are also supposed to have more facial hair than that."

"Okay fine!" Micha exclaimed impatiently. "I'm not with engineering. Just doing stuff."

"Well, okay then."

"Yup, okay then." Micha looked at Zach with the smile of irritation and waved at him. "Well, nice talking to you," Micha said as he turned his back toward Zach intending to continue his search.

Zach, successfully put off, turned to go when, suddenly, there was a massive bang, the ground shook, the air was filled instantly with dust and debris, and Micha and Zach were rendered unconscious.

After a short period, the dust began to settle. Debris was everywhere and both ends of the inner tunnel were caved in. There was no way in or out and there was no way of knowing what people were doing on the other sides. Simultaneously and soon after the explosion Micha and Zach both regained consciousness.

"Hey man. You okay?" Micha asked, looking at Zach. They slowly began to process their new surroundings, to survey their state, and to check in with one another.

"I think so. What in the world just happened?"

"I'm not sure. It looks like the steel wall just blew into the East Wing," Micha said. "I think if we were just a few feet more to the right, we would both be dead."

"You have got to be kidding me." Micha wiped

his eyes and pinched his arm to make sure he was not dreaming. "I can't believe it. That's it. It's the tunnel. Something must have just blown the wall in from the outside."

"Looks like the East Wing caved in both ways," Zach said. "And, it looks like there's no way out."

"No!" Micha exclaimed as his mind became fully awake and alert. "This is the tunnel out. It was a mistake during the construction of the *Network*. They dug the tunnel in the wrong place. This is the way out."

"What do you mean out?" Zach asked, with confused.

"It's the way out to the upside," Micha said, as he continued to gaze into the tunnel.

"What? The upside? Like the land of the synthetics? The s*yners*?"

"I think so. I can't believe this is actually happening. I've been waiting for this moment for as long as I can remember. I'm going up."

"Are you crazy?" Zach exclaimed. "You can't go up there. You don't know"—he grabbed Micha's shirt—"what's up there."

"Don't you want to find out?"

"Not really. Maybe I did once. But not anymore."

"Yeah me too, but now I'm just curious." Micha pulled his shirt out of Zach's hands. "Well, you can just wait here till they dig you out, but I'm going up."

"I don't want to stay here by myself," Zach said, with a very concerned tone.

"Then you better come with me. I'm going up."

Micha and Zach walked into the mistaken tunnel to a destination that almost no one in the *Network,* for centuries, had ever seen. They walked and climbed through rubble and broken rock at the entrance and in complete darkness as they proceeded through the tunnel.

As they progressed, Micha wondered what it was that could have caused the explosion. He thought it too unrealistic for it to be a simple accident and came to the conclusion that someone or something might be trying to get into the *Network* from the upside. Zach was wondering the same thing and trembled thinking that at any moment they could be face to face with someone from the upside. Nonetheless, they both concluded, in their minds, that they had come too far and their best chance for safety was to get out.

Several hours passed as their felt their way though the pitch-black tunnel until finally, a tiny light emerged. The closer they got to the light, the more the tunnel brightened.

"Looks like the opening to the tunnel is ahead," Micha said.

"Yay. Man, something really smells in here."

"It might be dead bodies."

"What? You're kidding right?"

"Just kidding…but not really." Micha chuckled.

"Actually, it kinda smells like really bad body odor mixed with eggs."

"You know I think you nailed that smell. That's totally what it smells like."

"My name is Zach Kelly by the way."

"Micha Jennings. And Zach, we are about to make history."

The two citizens of Salem appeared at the front of the tunnel and found a large steel door already open. Nearly paralyzed with apprehension, Micha inched to look outside the door.

"What do you see?" Zach asked.

Micha did not respond as he slowly walked out and witnessed a dirt path looking as if it led to the top of a small hill made of large broken rocks resembling a kind of quarry.

"Is that the sky?" Zach asked. "It's indescribable. It's nothing like the pictures I've seen."

"Yeah, and I think that is the sun. It kinda hurts my eyes to look at it."

"It almost feels like it's burning my skin," Zach added.

"It actually might be. And that smell. This must be what real air smells like." Micha smelled a mixture of trees and the ocean.

"What? Now how in the world can there be such a thing as fake air?"

"Never-mind. Did you feel that?" Micha felt a gust of wind blow across his body.

"Yeah it kinda felt like a fan blew on us."

"I think it's called wind."

"I like it. It smells good. It smells clean. If that makes any sense."

Micha pointed to the path that led to the top of the hill. "I guess we should follow the path."

"Just be careful."

As they reached the top of the hill they stood stunned and speechless. Their eyes were opened as wide as possible. Their mouths were opened wide, and Micha started breathing heavily as if hyperventilating. They stood speechless without the slightest movement as they both gazed upon a large city on the upside for the first time in their lives. They were in such shock that they did not realize that

CONCLUSION

a *syner* was standing behind them.

"Are you seeing what I'm seeing?" Zach asked, in utter amazement.

"I, I did not think men could build such things." Micha stood bewildered.

"What are we going to do?" Zach asked.

"I don't know."

For the first time in centuries, citizens of Salem stood on the upside. Micha and Zach continued to stand motionless as the wind blew and the glaring eyes of a *syner* were upon them.

FURTHER INFORMATION AND RESOURCES

www.CentralBaptistHawaii.org

www.JunkerJorg.com

Get additional books and e-book from Amazon.com

Soli Deo Gloria

Made in the USA
San Bernardino, CA
30 July 2018